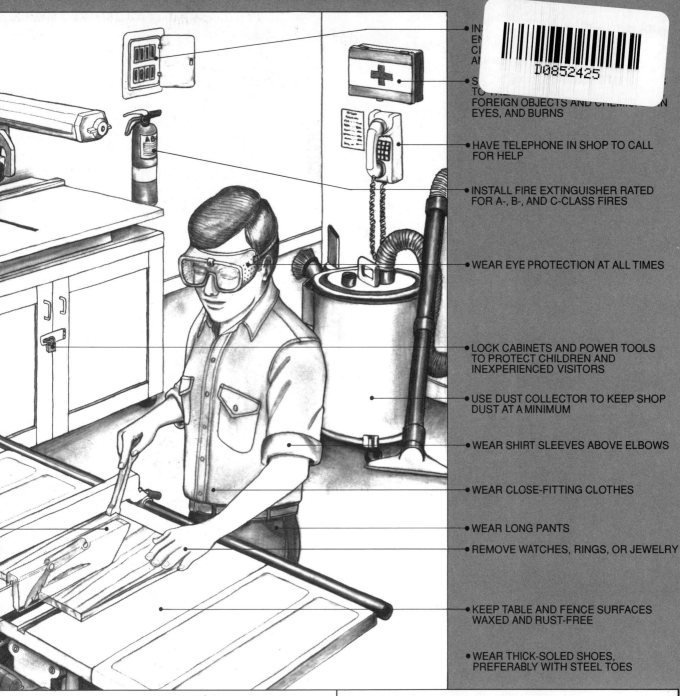

INS...
EN...
CH...
AN...

S...
TO...
FOREIGN OBJECTS AND CHEMIC... IN
EYES, AND BURNS

● HAVE TELEPHONE IN SHOP TO CALL
FOR HELP

● INSTALL FIRE EXTINGUISHER RATED
FOR A-, B-, AND C-CLASS FIRES

● WEAR EYE PROTECTION AT ALL TIMES

● LOCK CABINETS AND POWER TOOLS
TO PROTECT CHILDREN AND
INEXPERIENCED VISITORS

● USE DUST COLLECTOR TO KEEP SHOP
DUST AT A MINIMUM

● WEAR SHIRT SLEEVES ABOVE ELBOWS

● WEAR CLOSE-FITTING CLOTHES

● WEAR LONG PANTS

● REMOVE WATCHES, RINGS, OR JEWELRY

● KEEP TABLE AND FENCE SURFACES
WAXED AND RUST-FREE

● WEAR THICK-SOLED SHOES,
PREFERABLY WITH STEEL TOES

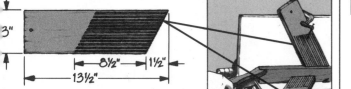

3"

8½" 1½"

13½"

CLAMP-ON FINGERBOARD

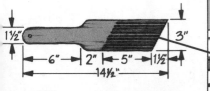

1½"

6" 2" 5" 1½"

3"

14½"

AND-HELD FINGERBOARD

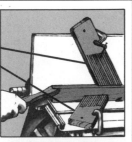

PROTECTION

WEAR FULL FACE SHIELD DURING LATHE
TURNING, ROUTING, AND OTHER OPERATIONS
THAT MAY THROW CHIPS

WEAR DUST MASK
DURING SANDING
AND SAWING

WEAR VAPOR
MASK DURING
FINISHING

WEAR SAFETY
GLASSES OR
GOGGLES AT ALL
TIMES

WEAR RUBBER
GLOVES FOR HANDLING
DANGEROUS CHEMICALS

WEAR EAR PROTECTORS
DURING ROUTING,
PLANING, AND LONG,
CONTINUOUS POWER
TOOL OPERATION

THE WORKSHOP COMPANION™

SHARPENING

TECHNIQUES FOR BETTER WOODWORKING

by Nick Engler

Rodale Press
Emmaus, Pennsylvania

Printed in the United States of America on acid-free ∞, recycled ♲ paper

If you have any questions or comments concerning this book, please write:
Rodale Press
Book Readers' Service
33 East Minor Street
Emmaus, PA 18098

About the Author: Nick Engler is an experienced woodworker, writer, and teacher. He worked as a luthier for many years, making traditional American musical instruments before he founded *Hands On!* magazine. Today, he contributes to several woodworking magazines and teaches woodworking at the University of Cincinnati. He has written more than 30 books.

Series Editor: Jeff Day
Editors: Bob Moran
          Roger Yepsen
Copy Editor: Carolyn Mandarano
Graphic Designer: Linda Watts
Illustrator: Mary Jane Favorite
Master Craftsman: Jim McCann
Photographer: Karen Callahan
Cover Photographer: Mitch Mandel
Proofreader: Hue Park
Indexer: Beverly Bremer
Typesetting by Computer Typography, Huber Heights, Ohio
Interior and endpaper illustrations by Mary Jane Favorite
Produced by Bookworks, Inc., West Milton, Ohio

Library of Congress Cataloging-in-Publication Data

Engler, Nick.
    Sharpening/by Nick Engler.
       p.   cm. — (The workshop companion)
    Includes index.
    ISBN 0–87596–584–9   hardcover
    1. Woodworking tools.   2. Sharpening of tools.   I. Title
    II. Series:
    Engler, Nick.   Workshop companion.
    TT186.E524   1994
    684'.08—dc20   93–37564
                                              CIP

2 4 6 8 10 9 7 5 3 1   hardcover

The author and editors who compiled this book have tried to make all the contents as accurate and as correct as possible. Plans, illustrations, photographs, and text have all been carefully checked and cross-checked. However, due to the variability of local conditions, construction materials, personal skill, and so on, neither the author nor Rodale Press assumes any responsibility for any injuries suffered, or for damages or other losses incurred that result from the material presented herein. All instructions and plans should be carefully studied and clearly understood before beginning construction.

Special Thanks to:

Richard Belcher
Dayton, Ohio

Grizzly Imports
Bellingham, Washington

Steve Taylor
Taylor Saw Shop
Brookville, Ohio

Wertz Hardware
West Milton, Ohio

Woodcraft
Parkersburg, West Virginia

CONTENTS

TECHNIQUES

PROJECTS

TECHNIQUES

1

A Sharpening Primer

The *first* thing I show new woodworking students, before they get busy with a project, is how to sharpen a chisel and a plane iron. We go through the steps together — grinding, honing, polishing, and buffing — then test the finished edges. Invariably, their eyes light up as the tools glide through long grain and end grain with equal ease, leaving a glass-smooth surface in the wood. Often for the first time, they experience the pleasure of working with a really sharp tool.

But in time, they invariably come up against a dull tool that can't be sharpened with the simple techniques they've been taught. At this point in their experience, sharpening is still a mysterious ritual in which they anoint a sharpening stone with honing oil and implore whatever minor deity handles such details to, please, let it be right this time. They know *what* to do, but not *why* they're doing it. Consequently, they can't improvise a solution for anything out of the ordinary.

So I go through the process again, this time explaining *how the tool cuts the wood.* As this revelation dawns, sharpening ceases to be a ritual to them and becomes just plain common sense. From then on, it's much easier to put a keen edge on a cutting tool.

HOW A TOOL CUTS WOOD

There is more to cutting wood than first meets the eye. To truly understand the process, you must get down to the microscopic level and study the relationship between the wood structure, the cutting edge, and the angle at which the tool meets the wood.

A DEFINITION OF CUTTING

Down at the level where the point of the cutting edge meets the individual wood fibers, cutting is synonymous with breaking — or *stress/failure,* to use the technical term. The point of the cutting tool presses against (stresses) the fibers with enough force that they break (fail), separating into two pieces. Cutting, in the parlance of engineers who design cutting tools, is a stress/failure process.

You don't necessarily need a pointed tool to stress the wood to the point of failure. You can break a board into two pieces with the blunt end of a hammer if you hit the board hard enough. However, this isn't cutting — it requires too much force and the broken edges will not be smooth.

A *cutting edge* concentrates all the force driving the tool at the point where two metal surfaces meet, called the *arris.* This point contacts only a small amount of the wood surface; consequently, the resistance to the force is confined to a tiny area and the force is concentrated, separating the wood easily. Furthermore, because the failure occurs along a narrow line described by the path of the cutting edge, the break is clean and even. The surface is cut smooth and doesn't appear broken. (SEE FIGURE 1-1.)

This simple experiment illustrates the principle. Poke two holes in a sheet of paper, one with the blunt end of a pencil and the other with the sharp end. It requires more force to drive the blunt end of the pencil through the paper, and the resulting hole is ragged. It's considerably easier to make a hole with the sharp end, and the hole is cleaner. (SEE FIGURE 1-2.)

A keen or *sharp* edge is one that has been ground and honed to an extremely fine point all along the arris. The finer the point (or the sharper the cutting edge), the smaller the surface area of the wood that it contacts. Sharper edges can be driven through wood with less force, and they leave smoother surfaces.

1-2 The holes in this piece of paper dramatically illustrate the value of a sharp point. The clean, round hole was made with the sharp end of a pencil, while the ragged, irregular hole was made with the blunt end.

1-1 The force required to drive a tool through a piece of wood is directly proportional to the amount of surface area it contacts. Because a sharp tool contacts a small surface area, only a small force is needed for it to cut. Furthermore, because this force is concentrated in a small area, the wood fibers will separate along a narrow line described by the path of the tool, and the cut surface will appear smooth and even. A blunt tool contacts a larger surface area and requires more force to cut. The fibers fail along a wider, poorly defined line, and the cut is ragged.

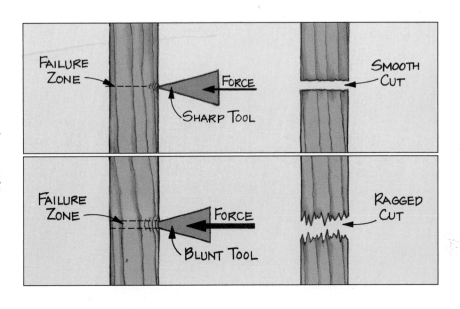

CUTTING-EDGE GEOMETRY

Sharpness isn't the only attribute of the cutting edge that affects the cut. The angle between the surfaces of the tool, the angle at which the edge attacks the wood, and the shape of the surfaces also determine how a tool cuts.

Every cutting edge has two surfaces. The surface that faces in the direction of the cut is the *leading face;* the opposite surface is the *trailing face.* The angle between these two surfaces is the *tool angle* — the smaller the tool angle, the less force it requires to cut with the tool. (*SEE FIGURE 1-3.*) However, if this angle is too small, the cutting edge will wear quickly. The more acute the tool angle, the less metal there is to buttress the cutting edge as you work. And if there is too little metal behind an edge, it breaks or dulls easily.

FOR YOUR INFORMATION

The tool angle is often confused with sharpness — novices think that the smaller the angle, the sharper the tool. This is not true — sharpness refers to the *condition* of the edge, not its angle. A router bit, for example, has a high tool angle, but when the point is crisp and keen, the edge is sharp.

When is the tool angle too small? That depends on the type of metal and how the tool is used. Generally, the harder the metal, the smaller you can grind the tool angle. However, hard metal is brittle, and an acute edge will break easily. Furthermore, metal has a granular structure, and different types of tool steel have different grain sizes. The coarser the grains, the coarser the cutting edge will be no matter what angle you use.

You can grind coarse steel to a small tool angle, but what good will it do since it won't take a sharp edge? (*SEE FIGURE 1-4.*) Refer to "Tool Steels and Carbides" on page 14 for more information on the characteristics of metal.

If they're made from good steel, light-duty tools can be ground to small tool angles; heavy-duty tools must have larger tool angles. Delicate carving tools that are

| **FINE-GRAIN STEEL** | **COARSE-GRAIN STEEL** |

1-4 The sharpness of a tool doesn't depend on the tool angle, but on the metal itself. Metal has a granular structure, and the size of the individual grains determines how sharp you can make a cutting edge. The finer the grains, the finer the point you can grind. This is why you can grind some types of tool steel sharper than others. It's also why you can't get carbide as sharp as good steel — carbide grains are larger than those in fine tool steel.

1-3 The two surfaces of a cutting tool come together in a crisp arris known as the *cutting edge.* The surface that faces the direction of the cut is the *leading face,* and the other is the *trailing face.* The angle between the two is the *tool angle.* The angle at which the leading face meets the wood — the *cutting angle* — is measured from an imaginary line perpendicular to the wood surface. The angle between the trailing face and the wood surface is the *clearance angle.*

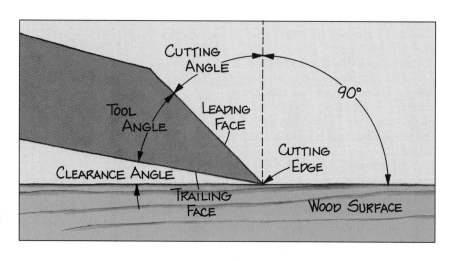

used only with light hand pressure are commonly sharpened at 15 to 25 degrees. Mallet-driven carving implements, woodworking chisels, and plane irons must withstand more abuse, and so are ground between 25 and 35 degrees. Jointer and planer knives, which are driven by powerful motors and slam into the wood several thousand times a minute, are sharpened at 35 to 45 degrees. And router bits and shaper cutters, because they rotate even faster than jointers, may be ground to still steeper tool angles.

The angle at which the cutting edge attacks the wood is called the *rake angle,* or *cutting angle.* This angle is measured between the leading face of the tool and a line drawn perpendicular to the surface of the work. More than any other angle, it determines how the tool cuts and how much force is required.

■ When a tool meets the wood at a *large* cutting angle, it lifts the chip and the wood fails *ahead* of the cutting edge. This type of cut requires the least force and produces a fairly smooth surface.

■ At a *moderate* cutting angle, the force required to make the cut increases. The tool compresses the chip and shears the fibers before it lifts the waste very far, and the failure occurs *near* or *at* the cutting edge. As long as the chip is fairly thin, the cut surface will be smooth.

■ When the cutting angle is very *small,* the force required is enormous. The tool compresses the wood without lifting it, and the wood fails erratically ahead of (and often below) the cutting edge. The resulting surface is rough with many torn wood fibers. *(SEE FIGURE 1-5.)*

A large cutting angle is best when cutting across the grain — it requires less force to sever the wood fibers, and the cut is generally cleaner. This is why a low-angle block plane is preferred for planing end grain — the plane iron is bedded at a low angle so the cutting angle is increased (53 degrees for a low-angle plane versus 45 degrees for a standard plane). A moderate cutting angle is better for cutting with the grain. The closer the wood fails to the cutting edge, the smoother the surface is apt to be.

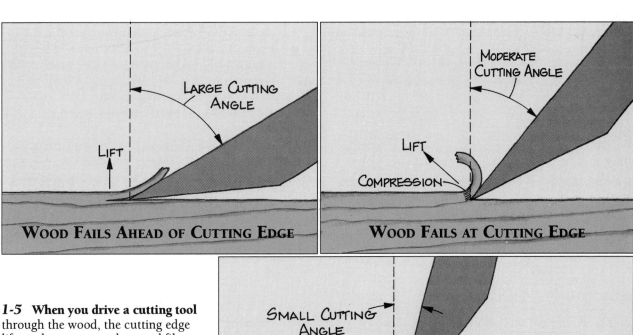

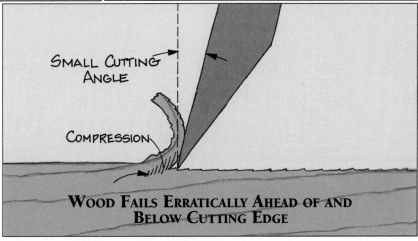

1-5 When you drive a cutting tool through the wood, the cutting edge lifts and compresses the wood fibers. At a large cutting angle, the lift is greater than the compression, and the wood fails ahead of the cutting edge. At a moderate cutting angle, the lift and compression are about equal, and the wood fails at the cutting edge. At a small cutting angle, there is more compression than lift, and the wood fails erratically ahead of and below the cutting edge.

FOR YOUR INFORMATION

Have you ever wondered why it's easier to cut with a bench plane if you hold it at an angle to the plane's direction of travel? When the plane is skewed this way, the effective geometry of the cutting edge changes, as shown in the drawing. The cutting angle increases, so the effort required to make the cut decreases. (By the way, skewing also works for woodworking chisels and carving tools.)

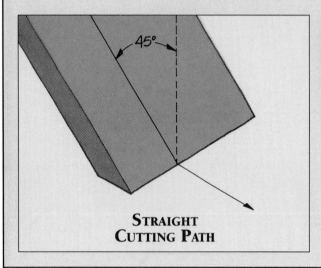

STRAIGHT CUTTING PATH

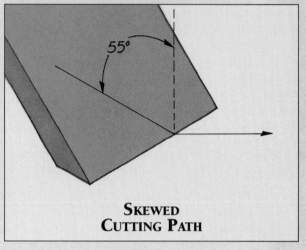

SKEWED CUTTING PATH

The angle between the trailing face of the tool and the work is the *clearance angle*. It's not important how large or small this clearance angle is, as long as there is one. Without a clearance angle, the point of the cutting edge will not contact the wood.

That sounds simple enough, but it's this clearance angle that gives many woodworkers fits. Until they learn proper sharpening techniques, novices tend to rock the chisel or the plane iron as they sharpen it, rounding the trailing face. When they rest the tool on the work with the bevel down and hold it at a normal cutting angle, the rounded face holds the cutting edge off the wood. For the cutting edge to contact the wood, the cutting angle has to be reduced. This, in turn, increases the force required to make the cut and reduces the quality of the cut surface. (*See Figure 1-6.*)

This isn't to say that the surfaces of cutting tools must always be ground and honed flat. The surfaces of chopping tools, such as axes and meat cleavers, are intentionally ground convex. This shape, called a *cannel grind*, increases the tool angle at the cutting edge and makes it more durable without increasing the overall thickness of the tool. The tool doesn't cut particularly smoothly, but the cutting edge stands up to heavy use.

The surfaces of some light-duty tools, such as razor blades, are ground concave. This *hollow grind* reduces the tool angle without decreasing the thickness of the tool. The cutting edge is incredibly thin, yet the tool remains stiff enough to hold its shape. However, the tool will not hold a sharp edge long or stand up to hard use.

For the most part, the surfaces of woodworking tools are ground flat. (*See Figure 1-7.*) A flat grind is reasonably durable, and it makes maintaining critical cutting and clearance angles easier.

WOOD STRUCTURE

Tool geometry is only half the story, however. The way in which a tool cuts is also determined by the nature of the wood itself. Wood is composed of long, tough *cellulose* fibers bound together with a weaker substance called *lignin*. The fibers are aligned in roughly the same direction, which gives the wood its characteristic grain pattern. As you drive a cutting edge into a workpiece, the wood can fail in two different ways — *along* the wood grain and *across* it. When the wood fails across the grain, the fibers break in two. When it fails along the grain, the fibers shear or split away from one another. (*See Figure 1-8.*)

Because cellulose is tougher than lignin, wood is a great deal stronger across the grain than along it — the fibers are more likely to split apart than to break.

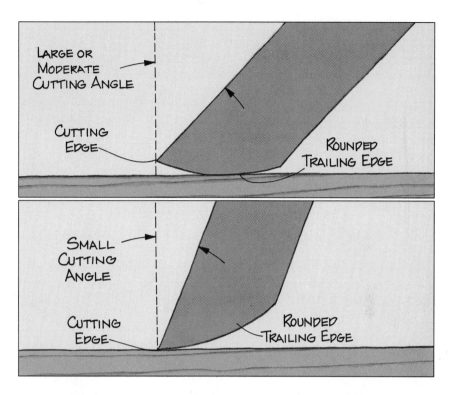

1-6 If you inadvertently round the trailing face as you sharpen a chisel, you increase the tool angle at the expense of the clearance angle. The cutting edge may not meet the wood when the tool is held at the proper cutting angle. You will have to reduce the cutting angle to cut with the chisel. This, in turn, increases the amount of force needed and reduces the quality of the cut.

1-7 There are three ways to grind the surfaces of a cutting tool — convex (*cannel* grind), concave (*hollow* grind), and flat. A cannel grind makes an extremely durable cutting edge, but the resulting tool angle is fairly high and the tool requires a great deal of force to cut. A hollow grind reduces the tool angle and makes it easier to cut, but the cutting edge isn't durable. The flat grind offers a good balance between cutting ease and durability.

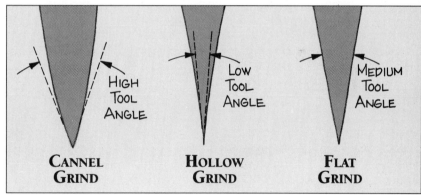

1-8 Wood grows in long cells, the walls of which are composed of tough *cellulose* fibers. The fibers are aligned and bound together with *lignin*. When you cut *along* the grain (parallel to the fibers), the lignin fails and the fibers separate from one another. When cutting *across* the grain, the cellulose fails, too, and the fibers separate. Because the cellulose fibers are stronger than lignin, it's easier to cut wood along the grain than across it.

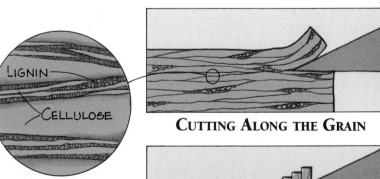

CUTTING ALONG THE GRAIN

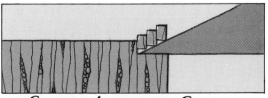

CUTTING ACROSS THE GRAIN

For this reason, it's easier to cut parallel to the grain than perpendicular to it. However, at a microscopic level, the wood often fails both ways — along the grain *and* across it — no matter what direction you're cutting.

For example, when you use a bench plane to surface a board, you're cutting roughly parallel to the grain. When the cutting edge of the plane iron enters the wood, it lifts a small chip. As the chip is pried upward, it splits along the grain, ahead of the cutting edge. It rides up the iron until the chip breaker turns the chip, breaking the fibers across the grain. The fibers aren't quite severed, however, and the chip rolls off the chip breaker in one long, curled shaving. *(See Figure 1-9.)*

When you use a mortising chisel to square the end of a mortise, you're cutting perpendicular to the grain. As the chisel enters the wood, the cutting edge severs the fibers across the grain. Then the tapered body of the chisel becomes a wedge, forcing the chip to one side. The fibers split along the grain, and the chip breaks into short segments. *(See Figure 1-10.)*

Rarely is the wood grain perfectly parallel or perpendicular to the path of a cut, however. Most of the time you must cut at a diagonal. If this is the case, it's always preferable to cut so the grain rises ahead of the cut rather than sinking down below it. When the grain rises ahead of the cut, you're cutting *with* the grain;

when it sinks ahead of the cut, you're cutting *against* the grain. *(See Figure 1-11.)* Cutting with the grain causes the wood to fail at or above the cutting edge — the cut surface is not damaged. Cut against the grain, and the wood fails below the cutting edge, tearing the fibers. Furthermore, because the tool wants to follow the path of least resistance — in this case, the gap that opens between the split fibers — the point tends to dig in, and a great deal of effort is required to keep it moving in the right direction. Consequently, cutting with the grain requires less effort and leaves a smoother surface than cutting against it.

The cutting process is also affected by those wood fibers in the vicinity of the cut that *don't* fail. Wood is *elastic*. If you strain it for a short period of time, hard enough to deform the fibers but not enough to break them, the wood will spring back to its original shape after the strain is released. Consider the bench plane again: As the iron enters the wood, it compresses the fibers ahead of it, much the same way a piece of bread is compressed when you cut it. As the fibers in the path of the blade fail, the strain that causes the compression is released. The fibers on either side of the cut — those that didn't fail — expand again. *(See Figure 1-12.)* This *springback* sometimes interferes with the accuracy and quality of a cut, particularly when the wood is soft or wet.

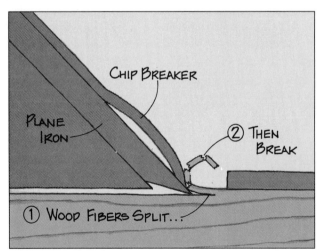

1-9 When you cut across the grain with a bench plane, the wood fails in two ways — *along* the grain, then across it. (1) As the cutting edge lifts the chip, the fibers split along the grain. (2) Then the chip rides up the plane iron and is turned by the chip breaker. As it turns, the fibers break *across* the grain.

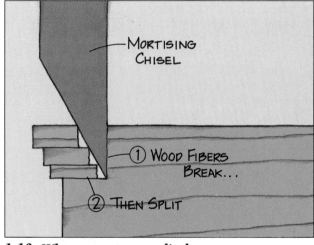

1-10 When you cut perpendicular to the grain with a mortising chisel, the wood also fails in two ways, but in the reverse order of the bench plane — across the grain, then along it. (1) As the chisel enters the wood grain, it severs the fibers across the grain, then (2) wedges the chip to one side so it splits along the grain.

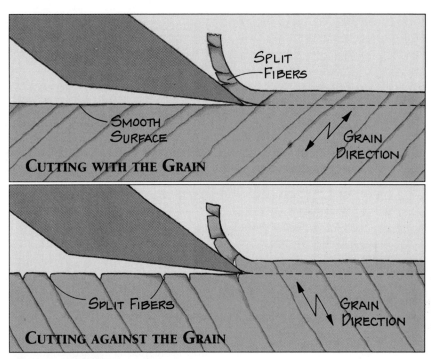

1-11 **When the wood grain *rises*** ahead of a cut, you're cutting *with* the grain. As the cutting edge lifts the chip, the fibers in it split. The cutting edge cleaves the fibers in the path of the cut, and the surface is cut smooth. When the wood grain *sinks* ahead of the cut, you're cutting *against* the grain. As the cutting edge lifts the chip, the fibers split below the path of the cut. This leaves a rough surface.

1-12 **The cutting edge of a bench** plane compresses the wood in its path. As the stock is cut and the edge passes by, the compressed wood springs back to its original shape. Consequently, the blade doesn't cut quite as deep as its depth setting. Usually, the springback is only a few thousandths of an inch, not enough to matter in most wood-working operations. But if the wood is soft or wet, or if the cutting edge is dull, then springback may become a problem.

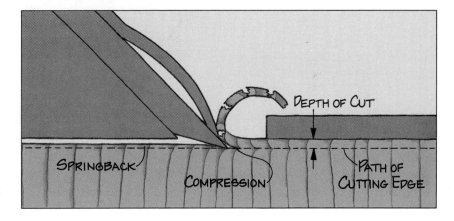

SHARPENING A DULL TOOL

WHY A DULL TOOL DOESN'T CUT WELL

As a tool is used, the sharp point of the cutting edge wears. The stress and strain associated with cutting cause microscopic fractures along the edge, blunting it. Extractives — tiny mineral grains embedded in the cell walls of the wood — abrade the edge and round it over. In some cases, the cutting edge may even bend or curl over, especially when the steel is soft and the tool angle is low. (*SEE FIGURE 1-13.*)

As these things happen, two things change:

■ The area of the tool that contacts the wood increases, and more force is required to drive the tool through the wood.

■ The relationship between the angles changes — the tool angle increases while both the cutting angle and the clearance angle decrease. (*SEE FIGURE 1-14.*) As this happens, the quality of the cut surface declines noticeably. (*SEE FIGURE 1-15.*)

A cutting edge may also accumulate tiny nicks and chips, particularly if it's made from hard steel or used to cut materials that it's not designed to cut. Nicks and chips also increase the surface area, thereby increasing the force required to make a cut. If they are large enough, the nicks leave lines of raised or torn fibers in the cut surface. (*SEE FIGURE 1-16.*)

If you suspect a cutting edge is growing dull, look at it under a bright light. Because the surfaces of a sharp tool come to a crisp point, the cutting edge reflects no light. But once the edge begins to round over, the surface reflects a line of light. Chips and nicks in the edge will show as spots of light. (SEE FIG-URE 1-17.) Also inspect the cut surfaces. A sharp tool leaves a clean, smooth cut; cut end grain should be slightly darker than the surrounding wood. If the cut surfaces appear fuzzy or milky, the tool is dull.

1-13 The photo on the left shows the freshly whetted cutting edge of a carving chisel. The crisp, razor-sharp edge will slice through the hardest wood with ease. After the chisel has been used hard for the better part of an hour, the edge becomes rounded and uneven, as shown on the right. It's now difficult to force the chisel through softwood.

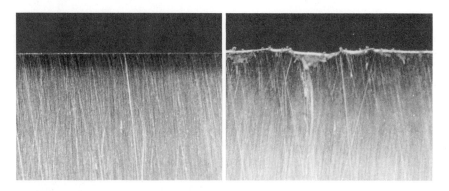

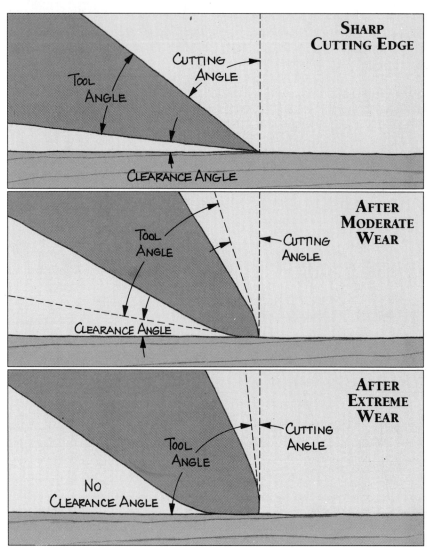

1-14 As a cutting edge grows dull with use, it rounds over — more on the trailing face than on the leading face. This changes the tool geometry. The tool angle increases, while the cutting angle and the clearance angle decrease. As this happens, more and more force is required to cut with the chisel, and the cut surface becomes rougher.

1-15 The cut end grain in this piece of ash demonstrates the difference in performance between a sharp chisel and a dull one. The end grain on the left was cut with a freshly sharpened chisel — the edges are crisp and the cut surfaces are smooth. The end grain on the right was cut with the same chisel after it had been used for the better part of an hour. The worn, dull cutting edge left rough, uneven surfaces. Close inspection shows that many of the wood fibers are mashed rather than cut.

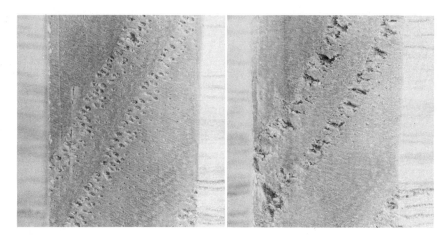

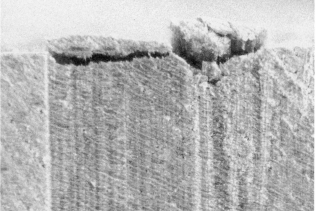

1-16 Nicks and chips in the cutting edges also ruin the quality of the cut. The board shown on the left was jointed with a set of nicked jointer knives. The nicks have left raised lines in the cut surface. The end of the board shown on the right was cut with a chipped chisel. Each chip has left a line of torn wood fibers.

1-17 If a tool isn't cutting as well as it might or if the cut requires too much force, inspect the edge under a bright light. A sharp edge (*left*) will reflect no light, but a dull one (*middle*) will show a line of light. Chips and nicks (*right*) in the edge will show up as dots of light.

RESTORING A CUTTING EDGE

Now that you know how a sharp tool cuts — and a dull one doesn't — it should be evident what you must do to sharpen it. As you can see, sharpening isn't a simple matter of grinding the cutting edge to a point. To restore a dull edge, you must accomplish three distinct goals.

First, restore the *geometry* of the tool — that is, grind the cutting edge to the proper tool angle. In many cases, you must also maintain the correct cutting and clearance angles. Use a honing guide or a tool holder of some sort to help do this. *(See Figure 1-18.)* You can get away without guides when you're just *touching up* a tool — honing or polishing a slightly worn cutting edge to restore the sharpness — because you don't remove much metal. But even experienced sharpeners will admit that they can maintain the tool geometry more precisely with a guide.

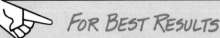

For Best Results

One of the most important sharpening secrets is to maintain the same *precise* tool angle throughout the sharpening process — not only as you rub the tool across a single stone but also as you go from stone to stone. *This is extremely critical* and is much easier to accomplish with a honing guide or a tool holder.

Second, grind the surfaces of the tool to the proper shape. For most woodworking tools, this means grinding the face and the bevel *flat. (See Figure 1-19.)* Even when sharpening the edges of curved tools such as gouges, remember that if you were to view a cross section of the cutting edge from the side, the leading and trailing faces should appear flat.

For Your Information

Some craftsmen prefer to "hollow grind" chisels and planes. However, this is not a true hollow grind as described in *Figure 1-7* but rather a presharpening technique that reduces the amount of time spent hand sharpening. The shape of the surfaces near the tips of the tools remains flat. For more information on this technique, refer to page 51.

Third, *finish* both the leading and the trailing faces. To create a sharp edge you must make a crisp, keen arris. When you sharpen, you remove metal from the faces with *abrasives*. If you only use coarse abrasives, the cutting edge will be rough. Instead, you must work your way through progressively finer abrasives, making the cutting edge sharper and sharper. *Grind* the faces with coarse abrasives to quickly remove the worn surfaces and restore the tool to its proper shape. Then *hone* the faces with medium abrasives to remove the deep scratches left by the coarse abrasives.

You can stop at honing for many machine cutters and heavy-duty hand tools, but fine hand tools require an extra step — *polishing* the faces with fine abrasive to make them truly smooth. Many craftsmen go a step further, *buffing* or *stropping* their tools to a mirror finish to create the keenest possible edge. *(See Figure 1-20.)*

1-18 A honing guide (shown) and other tool holders help maintain the proper tool geometry when you sharpen. They are particularly useful when you must grind away a large amount of metal to restore the tool to its proper shape. They also eliminate the natural tendency people have to rock the tool as they sharpen it, helping you to grind the surfaces flat. This particular type of guide also keeps the tool angle precisely the same as you work your way from coarse to fine abrasives.

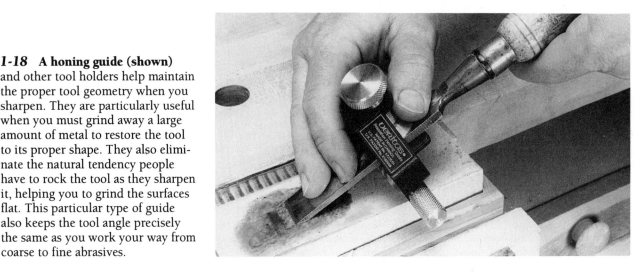

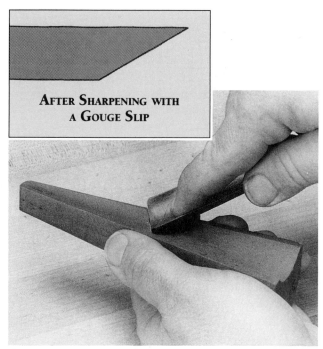

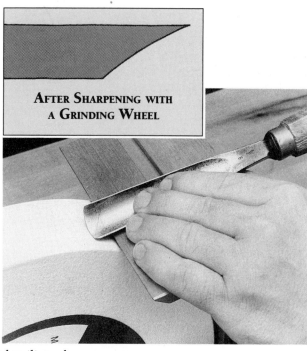

1-19 Carefully choose your sharpening tools to grind the surfaces of a cutting edge *flat*. Match the surface of the abrasive to the shape of the tool so that a cross section of the cutting edge will show a straight leading and trailing edge. Grinding wheels are round and will not produce a flat surface — these are best used to grind the rough shape of the cutting tool *before* sharpening.

1-20 When you inspect a cutting edge under a magnifying glass, you can see how the arris becomes sharper as you work your way up through finer abrasives. The photo on the upper left shows the edge of a chisel after it was *ground* with a coarse bench stone. The same chisel is shown on the upper right after it has been *honed* with a medium stone, then again on the lower left after being *polished* with a fine stone. The photo on the lower right shows the chisel after it was *buffed* with a buffing compound and a strop.

TOOL STEELS AND CARBIDES

How sharp an edge you can put on a tool and how well it retains its sharpness depends on what the tool is made of. Just as there are many species of wood that behave slightly differently when you cut them, there are many types of steel and carbide that behave differently when you sharpen and cut with them.

Tool Steels — At the molecular level, steel is a *crystal*. The crystals form *grains,* each grain .02 inches to .0001 inches in size. The smaller the grains, the sharper you can grind a cutting edge. The shape and composition of the crystals determine how hard and how tough the steel is. The grain size, composition, and geometry all depend on how the steel is made. The material undergoes several fiery reincarnations before it can be used for a cutting tool, and each reincarnation adds to its character.

Steel, of course, begins as iron ore and is refined to pig iron in a blast furnace. The pig iron is melted again in an atmosphere of pure oxygen to reduce *residual elements* (contaminants) such as carbon, silicon, and manganese. (Some, however, remain.) This makes *tonnage steel,* the stuff that bridges and car bodies are made of.

The tonnage steel is melted yet again and small amounts of other elements — chromium, vanadium, tungsten, and molybdenum — are added in varying proportions to make an alloy steel. The alloys and remaining residual elements (particularly carbon) begin to give the steel some backbone. For instance, tungsten and vanadium help keep the crystal grains small. Large amounts of carbon make it possible to harden the steel.

But even after three meltdowns, the alloy steel isn't especially hard. It's allowed to cool slowly (metallurgists say that the steel is *annealed*) and remains soft enough to be forged and ground into shape. The annealed crystal structure, called *ferrite,* is little different from tonnage steel. The carbon, alloy elements, and some of the iron have combined to make tiny, superhard particles of *carbide,* which are dispersed throughout the steel. These increase the resistance of the steel to wear, but don't contribute to its overall hardness.

The steel is usually rolled out while it cools. Rolling aligns the crystals and makes the steel tough. It's cut to size, reheated, and forged (hammered)

into a rough shape — a chisel, a plane iron, a planer blade, or what have you. Forging reduces the sizes of the crystals and increases their density, so the steel becomes tougher yet. Then it's ground to its final shape.

After shaping, it's heated again — not enough to melt the steel but enough to dissolve the alloys into the ferrite. This changes the ferrite into a denser crystal, *austenite.* If the steel cools slowly, the austenite will revert back to soft ferrite. So instead the steel is *quenched* — cooled rapidly with water, oil, or air. Not only does this preserve the alloys as part of the crystal structure but it also traps excess carbon atoms inside the crystals, transforming the material into yet another crystal form, *martensite.*

The quenched steel is extremely hard — too hard for its own good. Extremely hard steel is too brittle and likely to chip or break. So the steel is heated a final time, just enough to *temper* the cutting edge and relieve some of its hardness. Cutting tools are normally tempered to between 58 and 61 on the Rockwell C-Scale of Hardness. This makes them reasonably hard *and* tough. (Annealed tool steel is usually about 20 on the same scale and can be as hard as 70 immediately after quenching.)

After six baptisms by fire, the character of the steel has fully developed. Its specific traits depend on its hardness and composition — the proportions of carbon and alloy elements in the steel. The American Iron and Steel Institute (AISI) labels different compositions for different applications. For example, steels with high molybdenum content, such as AISI M2 and M4, resist heat and wear. They make good planer knives, router bits, and other high-speed cutters. (M2, M4, and other heat-resistant steels are often referred to as high-speed steels or HSS.) Most top-quality chisels and plane irons are made from AISI W2, W4, and other high-carbon steels. These take an exceptional edge and retain it well under relatively light loads.

Should you be concerned about the type of steel in a chisel? Yes and no. You cannot order a chisel made from a particular AISI recipe. Furthermore, the differences between grades of tool steel are so subtle that most woodworkers cannot detect them. The best you can do is to purchase tools of reasonable quality from reputable manufacturers and trust that the tools are made of good steel. However, don't be suckered into paying more for a tool because it's made of "high-carbon steel," "Sheffield steel," or the like. These are advertising gimmicks; they don't tell you anything about the quality of the materials or how a tool is forged or tempered. "Laminated steel" is another subterfuge. This simply means that the manufacturer has wedded a small amount of hard tool steel to a lot of soft, cheap steel and is probably asking you to pay more for it.

Carbides — The character of carbide isn't quite as complex as tool steel, perhaps because it only suffers through two fires. Like tool steel, carbide also has a granular structure. The individual grains are made by fusing iron, carbon, and an alloy metal (usually tungsten) in a furnace. Then these grains are fused together with a binding metal such as cobalt. The result is an extremely hard, brittle, and wear-resistant material. Most carbides are too brittle to be used for the plates or bodies of cutting tools, so just the cutting edges are tipped with carbide.

Like steel, the sharpness of a carbide cutting edge depends on the size of the individual carbide grains. Unfortunately, even the smallest carbide grains are larger than the crystals in a good tool steel, so carbide cutters cannot be sharpened to the same degree. The *only* advantage that carbide has over

steel is that the cutting edge stays sharp longer. This can be especially important in production woodworking or when you work with tough materials such as plywood or particleboard.

Carbide has a serious character flaw — it corrodes when exposed to acid. The tannic acid common to many wood species eats away the binding agent between the carbide grains, dulling the cutting edge. This can happen even if you don't use the tool often. Professional sharpeners sometimes hear stories from woodworkers who rout oak or cherry with carbide-tipped bits, put the bits away without cleaning them, then take them out several months later to find them as dull as butter knives.

What should you look for in a carbide or carbide-tipped cutting edge? Again, don't be misled by the type of carbide used or claims about hardness. Even the softest carbide is plenty hard for any normal woodshop operation. You should, however, look for fine grain — this will ensure a reasonably sharp edge. Also look for corrosion resistance, especially if you're not in the habit of cleaning the cutting tools every time you use them. Finally, you might give some thought to the quality of the cut. If you want a really fine cut, maybe you don't want carbide at all.

 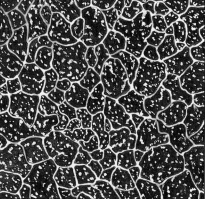 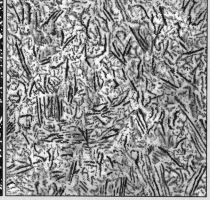

As tool steel is processed, the shape and size of its grains change, as these illustrations show. When it's first cast, the grain structure has a definite geometry and appears crystalline (*left*). When the steel has been forged and annealed, the grains become slightly smaller and their shape is less geometrical (*middle*). Finally, after hardening and tempering, the grains are much smaller and denser, appearing as tiny filaments (*right*).

2

Hand Sharpening Materials and Tools

When you hand sharpen a tool, you use an abrasive surface and a little elbow grease to grind away the rounded surfaces of a dull cutting edge, restoring it to a keen, crisp point. There are dozens of abrasive materials for hand sharpening — files, whetstones, buffing compounds, even sandpaper. There are also many tools to help you hold the cutting edge at a precise, constant tool angle and draw it out to a finer point.

What hand sharpening tools and materials do you need? That depends on the cutting tools you have to sharpen, your sharpening experience, and your personal preferences.

BENCH STONES

A set of whetstones or *bench stones* is at the center of most woodshop sharpening systems. *(SEE FIGURE 2-1.)* These are available in different sizes, shapes, materials, and abrasive grades or grit sizes. They are often sold in sets, including at least three grades — coarse, medium, and fine — to grind a cutting edge to a progressively finer point.

Many stones are used with oil or water. The liquid washes the stone's surface as you sharpen a tool to float away the metal filings, or *swarf,* so they won't *load* the stone. *(SEE FIGURE 2-2.)* On sharpening machines, liquids may also serve as a coolant, keeping the heat generated by abrasive friction from building up in the cutting edge. *(SEE FIGURE 2-3.)*

2-1 Five types of bench stones are commonly available in the United States. *Arkansas stones* (1) are natural stones mined in the Midwest. *Oilstones* (2), such as Crystolon and India, are synthetic stones made by bonding abrasive powders with resin or sodium silicate. Most *waterstones* (3) are also synthetic, made by bonding abrasives with clay. *Diamond stones* (4) aren't stones at all, but rather diamond dust imbedded in a steel plate. *Ceramic stones* (5) are created by fusing abrasives and ceramics at a high temperature. Refer to the chart "Sharpening Stones" on page 22 for a comparison.

2-2 When using most bench stones, you must spread a liquid on the surface as you sharpen. Oilstones require a light oil, waterstones need water, and Arkansas stones can be used with either oil or water. These liquids are *cleaners* that wash the abrasive and float away the metal particles, or *swarf*. Without the cleansing action of a liquid, the particles become impacted between the abrasive grains and keep the stone from grinding.

2-3 On some sharpening machines, liquids also serve as *coolants*. The faster the grinding action, the more heat is generated from abrasive friction. If the metal becomes too hot, it may lose some of its hardness and won't hold a sharp edge. When the moving stone is bathed in water or oil, the liquid helps dissipate this heat before it can affect the tool.

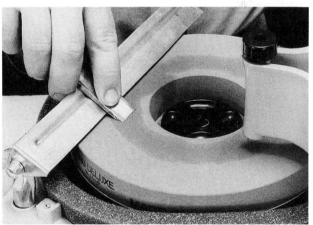

The materials used to make bench stones can be either natural or synthetic. Many types of natural sharpening stones were once imported from all over the world — Ayr stone, Turkey stone, snake stone, Norway ragstone, Cutler's greenstone, and so on. But these were gradually eclipsed by the high quality of whetstones found in just one location in the Midwest.

ARKANSAS STONE

Arkansas stone is the popular name for *novaculite,* which is mined in the Ouchita Mountains of Arkansas. It's a dense mass of quartz crystals, similar to flint except that the size of the crystals in each piece is extremely uniform. It's this unusual quality that makes the stone an extraordinary sharpening material.

Although the crystals are the same size in each piece, they do vary from piece to piece, creating several different grades of Arkansas:

■ *Washita,* a multicolored stone, is the coarsest. (Washita is a corruption of Ouchita.)

■ *Soft Arkansas* is the medium grade and is gray with green specks.

■ *Hard white Arkansas* has a fine grain.

■ *Hard black Arkansas* is ultrafine. It's sometimes referred to as *surgical stone* because medical and dental instruments are whetted on it.

Natural stones require some preparation before you first use them. Soak them in oil for a day or two or the porous material will absorb too much oil as you sharpen. Thereafter, keep the stones in a container to prevent the oil from evaporating and to protect them from dust. (*SEE FIGURE 2-4.*) If you don't use a stone for a long time and it dries out, soak it again before using it.

Why must you use oil with these stones and not water? You don't have to; water will do just fine. But water dries out quickly, and you must soak a dry stone before you can use it. In a pinch, you can use water on an oil-soaked stone, but it won't clean efficiently because water beads up on the oily surface.

Clean the stones by wiping away the dirty oil after you've finished sharpening. If a stone becomes extremely dirty or impacted with metal filings, clean it with oil or kerosene and a scrub brush.

2-4 Store oil-soaked Arkansas stones in covered containers to protect them from dust and to keep the oil from evaporating. Some craftsmen also place a piece of felt, soaked in oil, underneath the stones to keep them from drying. Despite some old wives' tales to the contrary, there is nothing special about the cedar boxes that the stones come in — it just happens that cedar is abundant in Arkansas.

Note: At present, all the known deposits of novaculite are being mined. As these mines are depleted, Arkansas stone will become increasingly scarce. In the not-so-distant future, there may be no natural stones available; *all* sharpening stones will be synthetic. Fortunately, some of the synthetics are just as effective and versatile as Arkansas.

SYNTHETIC OILSTONES

Synthetic oilstones are made by bonding abrasive grit with resin or sodium silicate. There are two common types:

■ *Crystolon* is made from silicon carbide and appears gray or black.

■ *India* is made from aluminum oxide and is brown, tan, or (occasionally) white.

Both of these materials are extremely hard and wear resistant — they retain their shape through heavy use. You may also find synthetic *Carborundum* stones, but avoid these. They are much softer than Crystolon or India, too soft to be used for even casual sharpening.

Crystolon and India are often used together in a single system — Crystolon for grinding, India for honing and polishing. They require no preparation unless specified by the manufacturer; the stones are usually oil-filled at the factory. They should be cared for in the same manner as Arkansas stones — use a light oil to float away the swarf; wipe away the dirty oil after each sharpening session; and clean them with oil and a scrub brush if they become dirty.

Note: The oil used with Arkansas stones and synthetic oilstones helps protect your tools from rust.

WATERSTONES

Japanese *waterstones* use water as a cleaner and coolant. There are both natural and synthetic waterstones. The natural stones are composed of compressed quartz, sericite, or volcanic ash. They are expensive and hard to come by because, after two thousand years of mining, the supply is very limited.

Only the synthetic waterstones are commonly available in the United States. They are made of silicon carbide or aluminum oxide bonded with clay. This clay is much softer than the bonding agents used to manufacture synthetic oilstones, and the abrasive wears away quickly. As you work, the grinding surface is constantly refreshed as new, sharp abrasive grains are exposed. The old, loose grains mix with the water to create an abrasive slurry, which aids the grinding. (*SEE FIGURE 2-5.*) As a result, the stones cut quickly. The drawback is that they also wear quickly and must be flattened often. (Refer to "Dressing Whetstones" on page 24.)

2-5 One of the major advantages of waterstones is that the abrasive grains on the surface wear away quickly, mix with the water, and form an abrasive paste that speeds the cutting action of the stone. However, exceptionally fine waterstones (6,000 and 8,000) are considerably harder than coarser stones, and it takes a long time to work up a paste. To create a paste on fine waterstones before sharpening, rub a *nagura stone* over the surface. Rub the entire surface so the stone wears evenly.

FOR YOUR INFORMATION

Some woodworkers think that waterstones cut finer than other sharpening materials because they have a smaller grit. However, this is not necessarily true. The Japanese grading system is different than the one used in the United States and creates the impression that the stones are finer. For example, a 1,000-grit stone in the Japanese system is equivalent to a 500-grit American. Even the finest waterstones, 8,000-grit Japanese, are only 1,200-grit on the American scale. Several other sharpening materials, including diamond and ceramic, are available in grits that are just as fine. You can purchase buffing and polishing compounds that are even finer.

Prior to using them, coarse and medium waterstones must be soaked in water for about 20 minutes or until they stop bubbling. Many craftsmen keep their waterstones submersed permanently so they're always ready for use, stored in plastic tubs with watertight lids. (*See Figure 2-6.*) Extremely fine waterstones are too dense to absorb much water and don't have to be soaked. Simply spray them with water as you use

them. Clean the stones by wiping away the slurry. Carefully dry the tools after you sharpen them on waterstones; otherwise, they may rust.

DIAMOND STONES

All of the whetstones covered so far — Arkansas stones, synthetic oilstones, and waterstones — will sharpen cutting tools made from hard, tough, high-carbon tool steels. They will *not*, however, sharpen carbide tools. Carbide is harder than the abrasive grains that the stones are composed of. To sharpen these tools, you need either diamond or ceramic stones.

Diamond bench stones are flat steel plates with diamond dust of a specific grit bonded to them. Oftentimes these plates are perforated with small holes and mounted to a plastic base. When used for hand sharpening, diamond abrasive plates don't require liquid cleaners or coolants. Clean them as you work by brushing or wiping away the filings. (*See Figure 2-7.*)

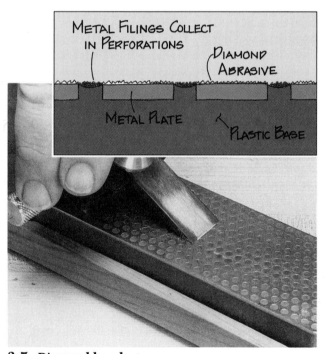

2-7 Diamond bench stones require no liquids because the filings don't become impacted between the abrasive grains. Simply brush or wipe off the metal dust. On perforated plates, the filings collect in the holes. This allows you to work for longer periods of time before you must clean the plate.

2-6 If you wish, store your waterstones submerged in covered plastic tubs so they're always ready to use. Change the water every few months to keep algae from forming. (To slow the growth of algae, add a few drops of chlorine bleach to the water.) Keep the tubs in a heated room to prevent the water from freezing.

CERAMIC STONES

Ceramic stones are manufactured from aluminum oxide grit, fused in a ceramic medium at an extremely high temperature. They are black or white in color and very hard. The fused abrasive grains are not as hard as diamonds; consequently, they are not the preferred material for sharpening carbide cutting tools. But they will grind through everything else with ease and tackle carbide if enough elbow grease is applied. Unfortunately, they are not available in coarse grits, so they cannot be used to grind metal quickly. They are best used for honing, polishing, and touching up cutting edges. (SEE FIGURE 2-8.)

Like diamond stones, ceramics don't require liquids.

The stones are not porous, so they don't load — the filings simply brush off. When a ceramic stone gets dirty, clean it with scouring powder, water, and a rag. Some craftsmen wipe ceramic stones with a damp cloth every now and then as they use them.

STONE SHAPES

All of these stones come in a variety of shapes and sizes for sharpening various cutting tools (SEE FIGURE 2-9):

■ Long, flat *rectangular* stones are used for sharpening flat chisels and plane irons.

■ Smaller *slip stones* have a rounded edge, a pointed edge, and two broad, flat surfaces. They are used for sharpening and touching up all types of chisels, knives, and carving tools. They can also be used to touch up jointer and planer knives without dismounting the cutters.

■ *Gouge slips* have two curved surfaces, one concave and the other convex. They also taper from one end to the other. As the name implies, they are used to sharpen gouges.

■ Stone *files* are long, slender rods that come in various shapes — round, square, triangular, and teardrop. They will sharpen or touch up small and intricately shaped cutting edges such as carving chisels, drill bits, and saw teeth.

2-8 Ceramic stones sometimes warp as they cool. Reputable manufacturers inspect and discard most of the warped stones, but a few slip through. Unfortunately, these stones are so hard they cannot be flattened in a home workshop. If you purchase a ceramic stone, check the surface with a precision straightedge before you use it. If it's warped, send it back and ask for a replacement.

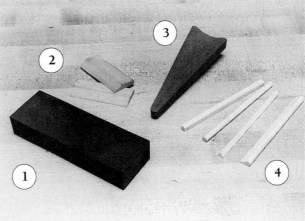

2-9 Sharpening stones come in a variety of shapes and sizes to reach the cutting surfaces of different tools. The most common shapes are long, flat *rectangles* (1). *Slip stones* (2) have round and tapered edges. *Gouge slips* (3) have concave and convex surfaces, and stone *files* (4) come in flat, round, triangular, and teardrop cross sections.

TRY THIS TRICK

Grind pieces of Arkansas and oilstone to any shape you want on a diamond bench stone. Use a coarse diamond stone to create the rough shape, then smooth the surfaces with finer grades.

SHARPENING STONES

TYPE OF STONE	ABRASIVE MATERIAL	BONDING AGENT OR PROCESS	AVAILABLE GRADES (U.S. GRIT)	COLORS
Arkansas Stones	Novaculite (quartz)	Geologic heat and compression	Washita (350)	Multicolored
			Soft Arkansas (500)	Gray with green specks
			Hard white (700)	White
			Hard black (900)	Black
Synthetic Oilstones	Aluminum oxide (India) and silicon carbide (Crystolon)	Resin, sodium silicate	Coarse India (100)	Brown or tan
			Coarse Crystolon (100)	Gray or black
			Medium Crystolon (180)	Gray or black
			Medium India (240)	Brown or tan
			Fine India (280)	Brown or tan
			Fine Crystolon (280)	Gray or black
Waterstones	Aluminum oxide or silicon carbide	Clay	250 Extra coarse (180)	Tan, brown, or gray
			800 Coarse (400)	
			1,000 Medium coarse (500)	
			1,200 Medium (600)	
			4,000 Fine (900)	
			6,000 Extra fine (1,000)	
			8,000 Ultrafine (1,200)	
Diamond stones	Diamond dust	Nickel (or another soft metal) fused to a steel plate	Coarse (240)	Silver gray; plastic bases are often color coded to help identify grades
			Medium (320)	
			Fine (600)	
			Extra fine (1,200)	
Ceramic stones	Aluminum oxide	Ceramics, fused at 3,000°F	Medium (600)	Gray
			Fine (1,000)	White
			Ultrafine (1,200)	White

TRY THIS TRICK

Using spray adhesive, stick sheets of aluminum oxide or silicon-carbide sandpaper to finished hardwood blocks to create a versatile, low-cost sharpening system. Use 120-grit for coarse, 220 for medium, 320 for fine, and 600 for ultrafine. These abrasives need no lubricants, although you can use water with wet/dry silicon-carbide sandpaper. When the abrasive becomes worn or loaded, simply peel up the old sheet and stick down another.

CLEANER/ COOLANT	PREPARATION	CARE	SPECIAL CHARACTERISTICS
Light oil or water	Soak in cleaner/coolant prior to using first time	Wipe away dirty oil or water after each use; cover stone to keep from drying; scrub clean with oil or kerosene	Long wearing; produces an extremely keen edge; oil helps to protect tools
Light oil	None required	Wipe away dirty oil after each use; scrub clean with oil or kerosene	Extremely hard and long wearing; inexpensive; produces serviceable edge; oil helps to protect tools
Water	Soak coarse and medium stones in water prior to using	Rinse stones after each use; if stones are stored submerged, change water occasionally and keep from freezing	Many grades available; fast cutting; produces extremely keen edge; wears quickly; must be flattened more frequently than other stones; water may rust tools
None required	None required	Brush away filings; wipe occasionally with damp cloth	Extremely long wearing; stays flat; produces keen edge; can be used to sharpen carbide; very expensive
None required	None required	Wipe occasionally with damp cloth; scrub clean with soap and water	Extremely long wearing; stays flat; produces extremely keen edge; no coarse grits available; can be used to sharpen carbide; moderately expensive

DRESSING WHETSTONES

The surfaces of most sharpening materials — Arkansas stone, Crystolon, India, and waterstones — wear away as you use them. After a time, they are no longer flat; they become concave or *dished*.

When this happens, it's impossible to grind a straight cutting edge. The stones must be *dressed* flat again.

1 **Dress Arkansas stones,** Crystolon, and India on a thick, flat metal plate called a *lapping plate*. (You can have a lapping plate milled from soft steel or cast iron at a machine shop.) Spread the plate with silicon-carbide powder or paste, available from automotive-supply stores (as *valve-grinding compound*) and lapidary-supply stores. Rub the surface of the stone back and forth across the plate, grinding it flat. Use a grit that's coarser than the stone itself to remove the concavity, then finish with a similar grit to smooth the surface. **Note:** You can also dress these materials on a diamond benchstone, provided the diamond stone is somewhat larger than the stone you want to flatten.

2 **Dress waterstones with** ordinary wet/dry sandpaper or sanding screen. Stick the sandpaper to 1/4-inch-thick plate glass with spray adhesive to hold it perfectly flat. Then rub the stone back and forth over the sandpaper. Use a generous amount of water to float away the waste. Again, start with a grit that's coarser than the stone and finish with a grit that's similar.

FILES, STROPS, AND GUIDES

Although bench stones are indispensable, there are many other helpful tools and materials for hand sharpening.

FILES

Files, although made of steel, are hardened to a much higher degree than most cutting tools. Consequently, they will easily cut away the worn surfaces of a cutting edge.

Files are available in three different grades. The coarsest is called a *bastard cut,* followed by *second cut* (medium) and *smooth* (fine). They also come in either of two tooth patterns. The teeth of *single-cut* files appear as parallel rows, while *double-cut* files have a crosshatch pattern. Most files made for sharpening are either second cut or smooth and have a single-cut tooth pattern. (If ever there was an industry in need of updated terminology, it's the file-making business. Try walking into a hardware store and ordering a second-cut, single-cut file. Chances are the clerk will just stare until you explain you're after a medium-grade file with parallel teeth.)

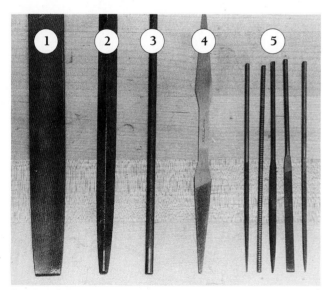

2-10 **The many shapes and sizes** of files made for sharpening tools include: a *mill file* (1) for general sharpening, a *three-square file* (2) for saw teeth, a *round file* (3) for hook teeth and chain saws, an *auger file* (4) for augers and drills, and *needle files* (5) for small and intricately shaped cutting tools.

Sharpening files also come in several shapes *(SEE FIGURE 2-10):*

■ *Mill* files are long, flat, and rectangular with a taper toward the end. They're used for sharpening axes, squaring scrapers, jointing saws, and general metalwork.

■ *Three-square* or *triangular* files have three sides and taper all along the length. They're designed to sharpen saw teeth and small cutting tools.

■ *Round* files are long cylinders, made for gouges, hook teeth, and chain saw teeth.

■ *Auger* files have flat, tapered surfaces at both ends. On one end, the edges are cut with teeth. On the other, the edges are *safe* — they have no teeth. This allows you to work in a corner without cutting both surfaces. These files are specially designed to sharpen drill bits and small cutting tools.

■ *Needle* files are small and slender and come in many shapes. Some have safe edges or faces; others have teeth cut in all surfaces. They're used to sharpen all manner of small tools and cutting edges with intricate shapes.

Treat these files as you would a good chisel — protect the cutting edges and don't just toss them in a drawer together. When the teeth become loaded with metal filings, clean them with a file card.

STROPS

Strops are flat, porous surfaces that can be loaded with ultra-ultrafine abrasive pastes and compounds. They are used like sharpening stones to polish and buff cutting edges to an extremely fine point. Traditionally, strops are made of leather and backed with wood, but the popularity of this design is declining. Leather gives when you press the edge of a tool against it, rounding the cutting edge slightly if you press too hard. Many craftsmen have gotten better results with strops made of hard cork or a close-grained hardwood, such as maple or basswood, jointed flat. *(SEE FIGURE 2-11.)*

There are several types of abrasives that you can apply to a strop:

■ Mix *pumice* or *rottenstone* with water or oil to make a thin paste. Spread this on the strop and let it soak in. **Note:** Rottenstone will produce a brighter polish and a finer edge than pumice.

■ Make a paste with *silicon-carbide powders* and apply it to the strop. These powders are available from automotive-supply stores (as valve-grinding

2-11 *Strops* **are used to polish** and buff cutting edges to extremely fine points. To use a strop, first apply a *small* amount of a fine abrasive paste or compound to make a light, even coating. If you're using a strop made from a soft material such as leather, rub the tool across it in the *opposite* direction in which the cutting edge is pointed — this will prevent the tool from cutting the strop. If using a strop made from hardwood, you can rub the tool back and forth as you would a sharpening stone. Refer to "Hand Sharpening Aids" on page 28 for instructions on how to make a wooden strop.

compound) and lapidary-supply stores. You also can buy ready-mixed paste.

■ Spread *buffing compounds* on the strop. These compounds are powdered corundum (a mineral related to the ruby) or other natural abrasives in a soft material such as wax or tallow. They come in three different grades. *Emery compound* is the coarsest, followed by *tripoli* (medium) and *jeweler's rouge* (fine).

■ Apply *polishing compounds* or *honing compounds* to the strop. These are similar to buffing compounds, except that they're composed of different types or grades of synthetic abrasives, such as chromium oxide. They may also cost more.

A little of these fine abrasives goes a long way. You don't need to load a strop every time you use it — just when it begins to take noticeably longer to polish a cutting edge. A single application may last for a week or more of *heavy use*. A two-pound bar of tripoli can easily last you the rest of your life. (You'll probably bequeath most of it to your children, who will have no use for it since they'll be cutting synthetic wood with lasers.) If you overload a strop, or wish to change to another compound, clean the strop with a wire brush or a *rake*. (*SEE FIGURE 2-12.*) Or if you're using a wood strop, scrape or sand the surface to reveal fresh wood.

2-12 **To clean a strop, simply** scrape the abrasive off the surface with a *rake*. You can buy commercial rakes, but there's little sense in it, since there are plenty of implements in your shop that will do just as well. A blunt knife, an old scraper (shown), and a used hacksaw blade all make excellent rakes.

HONING GUIDES

As mentioned in the previous chapter, *honing guides* help hold cutting tools — particularly chisels and plane irons — at precise angles to bench stones and strops as you sharpen. Some woodworkers condescendingly refer to these as "training wheels," but they are much more than that. Honing guides are nearly indispensable to good sharpening technique. Because most woodworking is now done with power tools, even experienced craftsmen may not sharpen enough hand tools to get the knack of holding an

angle. And even if you acquire the knack, these simple mechanical devices can do it better. Any professional sharpener will tell you the same.

A honing guide clamps the blade of a chisel or a plane iron in a holder so the bevel rests on the stone, supported by a rear wheel or roller. (*SEE FIGURE 2-13.*) To adjust the angle at which the chisel meets the stone, change the position of the blade in the holder. (*SEE FIGURE 2-14.*)

2-13 Most honing guides follow the same general design, but the rear support wheel may run either on the stone or off it. Each type has its advantages. With the rear support off the stone, you avoid rolling the iron filings into the abrasive. However, you must carefully readjust the tool angle every time you change stones — even slight variations in the stone's thickness will change the angle at which the tool is held. But when the rear support is on the stone, you can change from one stone to another without worrying about the thickness of each stone.

2-14 To adjust the tool angle when using a honing guide, change the position of the blade in the holder. For a smaller angle, extend more of the blade in front of the holder. For a larger angle, retract the blade. With some honing guides, you can also adjust the tool angle by changing the position of the rear support.

HAND SHARPENING AIDS

These simple jigs help to hand sharpen tools to a keener edge at a precise angle. A *honing guide* holds a chisel or a plane iron at a constant angle as you sharpen, and a *magnetic protractor* lets you set that angle accurately. A wooden *strop* polishes the leading and trailing faces to a mirror finish, drawing the cutting edge out to the sharpest possible point.

1 **To use the honing guide,** simply insert the blade of a chisel or a plane in the holder with the bevel down and tighten the wing nuts. Rest the bevel and the rear support wheel on the sharpening stone. Adjust the tool angle by moving the blade in the holder. When the angle is correct, push the chisel and the honing guide back and forth along the stone.

2 **To grind a bevel to a precise** angle, you must measure the angle of the blade in the holder. Rest the magnetic protractor on the surface of the stone and adjust the position of the scale so the wire pointer indicates 90 degrees. Then attach the magnetic protractor to the blade, as shown. Read the angle where the pointer crosses the scale.

3 **To make a wooden strop, cut** a thick board of close-grained basswood or maple across the grain to make ⅛-inch-thick slices. Arrange these slices edge to edge, with the end grain up, and glue them to a scrap of plywood. (By using the end grain as the stropping surface, you reduce the tendency of the cutting edge to dig into the wood.) Sand the surface flat on a sheet of sandpaper stuck to a glass plate, then check it with a straightedge. To seal and harden the surface, apply tung oil or Danish oil, then sand with fine wet/dry sandpaper while the oil is still wet. Wipe off the excess oil.

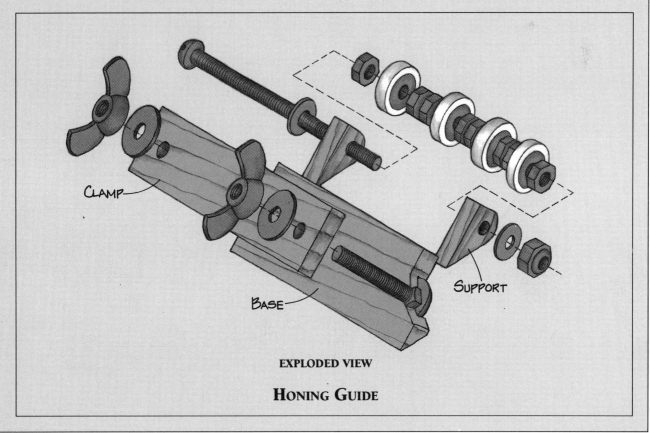

EXPLODED VIEW

HONING GUIDE

(continued) ▷

HAND SHARPENING AIDS — CONTINUED

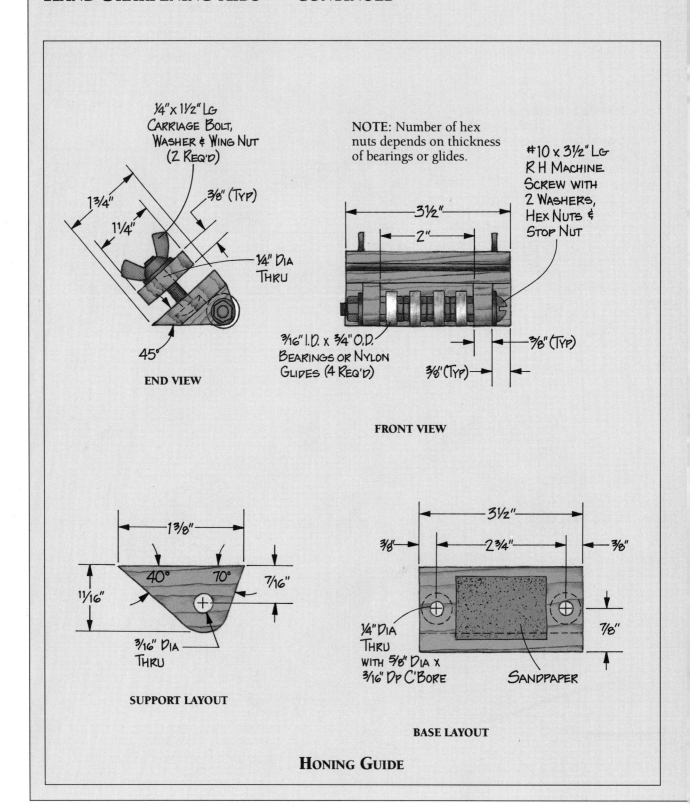

¼" x 1½" LG
CARRIAGE BOLT,
WASHER & WING NUT
(2 REQ'D)

3/8" (TYP)

1¾"

1¼"

¼" DIA
THRU

45°

END VIEW

NOTE: Number of hex
nuts depends on thickness
of bearings or glides.

#10 x 3½" LG
R H MACHINE
SCREW WITH
2 WASHERS,
HEX NUTS &
STOP NUT

3½"

2"

3/16" I.D. x ¾" O.D.
BEARINGS OR NYLON
GLIDES (4 REQ'D)

3/8" (TYP)

3/8" (TYP)

FRONT VIEW

1 3/8"

40°   70°

7/16"

11/16"

3/16" DIA
THRU

SUPPORT LAYOUT

3½"

3/8"   2¾"   3/8"

¼" DIA
THRU
WITH 5/8" DIA x
3/16" DP C'BORE

SANDPAPER

7/8"

BASE LAYOUT

HONING GUIDE

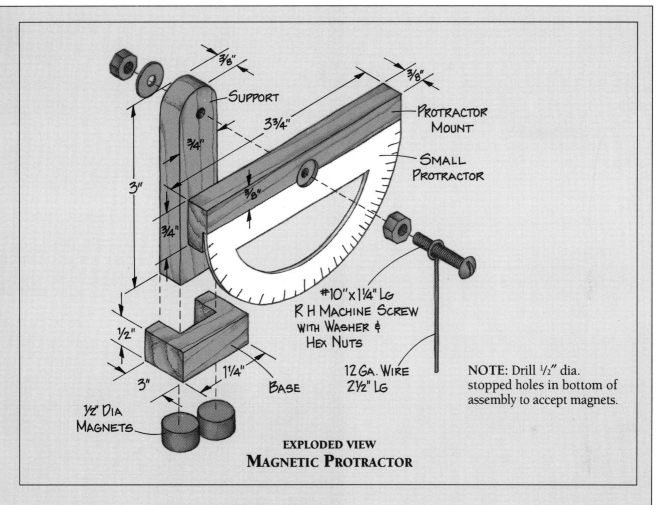

3/8"

SUPPORT

3/8"

PROTRACTOR
MOUNT

3 3/4"

SMALL
PROTRACTOR

3/4"

3"

3/8"

3/4"

#10" x 1 1/4" LG
R H MACHINE SCREW
WITH WASHER &
HEX NUTS

12 GA. WIRE
2 1/2" LG

NOTE: Drill 1/2" dia.
stopped holes in bottom of
assembly to accept magnets.

1/2"

3"

1 1/4"

BASE

1/2" DIA
MAGNETS

EXPLODED VIEW
MAGNETIC PROTRACTOR

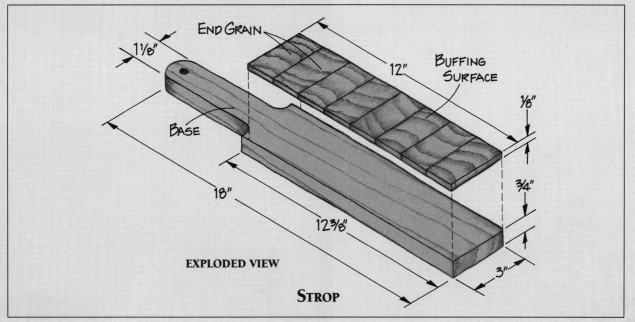

END GRAIN

1 1/8"

12"

BUFFING
SURFACE

1/8"

BASE

18"

3/4"

12 3/8"

3"

EXPLODED VIEW

STROP

3

SHARPENING AND GRINDING MACHINES

If you sharpen your tools often, or will be regrinding the shapes or angles, you may want the convenience of a power sharpener or grinder. These machines quickly remove metal, shaping the cutting edge and creating the desired geometry. Many machines will also hone and polish, sharpening the edge to a fine point.

There are several types of sharpeners and grinders commonly available, including bench grinders, buffing heads, wet grinders, motorized whetstones, and abrasive belt sanders. These can be organized in just two categories — hollow grinders, which grind a concave surface, and flat grinders, which leave a flat surface.

HOLLOW GRINDERS

Hollow grinders hold abrasive *grinding wheels* vertically, so that the work is ground on the circumference or edge. Because the grinding surface is curved, the work is hollow ground. There are two types of hollow grinders — dry and wet.

A SAFETY REMINDER

You can grind a flat surface on a grinding wheel by holding the work against the side, but this is dangerous on an ordinary grinding wheel. If there is a crack or a flaw in the wheel, the pressure from the side may cause the wheel to break up, throwing sharp chunks in every direction. Even if the wheel is solid, you might undercut the edge, causing the same spectacular explosion. If you must side grind, do so with wheels specifically designed for this operation.

DRY GRINDERS

There are two types of dry grinders — *bench grinders* and *buffing heads.*

A **bench grinder** is commonly used to grind rough edges on axes, shovels, lawn mower blades, and the like. It can also be used to grind metal to shape when making or repairing tools. It's not especially useful for sharpening fine woodworking tools, but it will let you perform a related task: You can hollow grind the bevel of a tool *before* sharpening it. By itself, a bench grinder will *not* put a sharp edge on a tool — the commonly available grades of dry grinding wheels are too coarse for honing and polishing.

Most bench grinders are simple machines — just motors, really — that turn wheels 6 to 8 inches in diameter. *(SEE FIGURE 3-1.)* The wheels are shielded, and tool rests support the work while grinding. *(SEE FIGURE 3-2.)* The less-expensive machines run at 3,450 rpm, much too fast for grinding steel cutting tools. At this speed, the heat from abrasive friction builds up so fast that the cutting edge will overheat in seconds. If the steel gets too hot, it will reduce the hardness and the tool will not hold a sharp edge as well.

To prevent this, you must touch the work lightly to the wheel, retract it almost immediately, wait a few seconds for the metal to cool, and repeat. Many craftsmen dip the tool in water as they grind. This not only cools the metal but it also helps them to tell when the tool is getting too hot. When the beads of water near

the cutting edge start to evaporate, it's time to back off. Unfortunately, these grind-a-little, wait-a-little techniques waste time and make it difficult to hold an accurate angle. It's better to invest in a low-speed grinder or to make your own (plans and instructions are on page 86).

FOR YOUR INFORMATION

If you come across an old *belt-driven* grinder, you can change the pulleys to run at any speed you want. Unfortunately, these machines are no longer commonly available.

When purchasing grinding wheels for a dry grinder, consider these characteristics *(SEE FIGURE 3-3):*

■ The *grit* should be between 60 and 100. Coarser grits scar the metal; finer grits run too hot unless you have a low-speed machine.

3-1 Dry bench grinders hold grinding wheels vertically, turning them so you can grind on the circumference of your work. They usually mount two wheels, with different grits or differently shaped edges. They commonly rotate *toward* the cutting edge as you hold the tool on the tool rest, and this limits the type of wheels you can mount on the arbors. You can safely mount grinding wheels and wire wheels, but *not* buffing wheels.

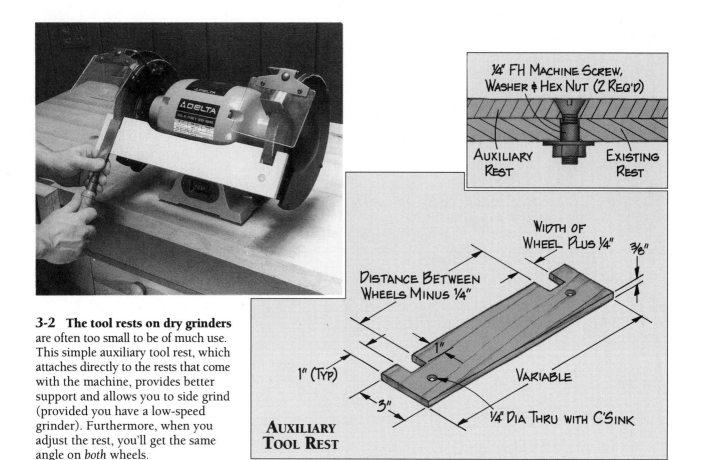

3-2 The tool rests on dry grinders are often too small to be of much use. This simple auxiliary tool rest, which attaches directly to the rests that come with the machine, provides better support and allows you to side grind (provided you have a low-speed grinder). Furthermore, when you adjust the rest, you'll get the same angle on *both* wheels.

■ The *bond* that binds the abrasive grain together should be either *vitrified* (ceramic) or *silicate*. Vitrified wheels can be used wet or dry; silicate wheels are made for dry grinding only.

■ The *bond grade* is rated from A (softest) to Z (hardest). Soft bonds grind cooler, and hard bonds wear longer. Somewhere between H and L gives you a good balance.

■ The *structure* refers to the density of the abrasive grains and is rated from 1 (dense) to 15 (open). A denser structure grinds smoother but hotter, and an open structure grinds quicker and cooler. Between 5 and 8 is a good choice.

■ The *maximum rpm* is the highest safe speed for the grinding wheel. The speed of your grinder should not exceed this number. It can be very dangerous to mount a low-speed wheel on a high-speed grinder — the wheel will break apart.

Buffing heads also have two arbors, but they don't have a built-in motor, guards, or tool rests. They are belt driven and designed to mount buffing wheels. (*See Figure 3-4.*) To use the buffing head, load the wheels with an abrasive buffing compound (if needed), then

3-3 The characteristics of a grinding wheel are indicated on the label. On this particular wheel, "A" refers to aluminum oxide, the type of abrasive, and "80" is the grit. "H" is the bond grade and "8" is the structure. "V" indicates the bond is vitrified, and the remaining letters are manufacturer's symbols.

3-4 Buffing heads are belt driven and rotate *away* from the cutting edge so you can safely mount buffing wheels. Use a 1,725-rpm motor and arrange the pulleys to turn the buffing wheel *no faster* than the motor speed. The motor pulley should be the same size or slightly smaller than the drive pulley.

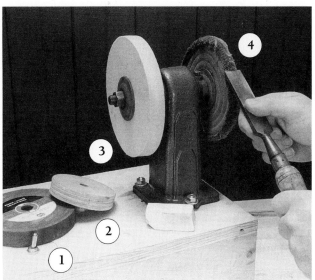

3-5 To use the buffing head, you must first mount buffing wheels on the arbors. There are four types commonly available — *rubber-bonded abrasive* (1), *leather* (2), *felt* (3), and *cloth* (4). Cloth, felt, and leather wheels must be loaded with abrasive buffing or polishing compounds; rubber-bonded wheels are already impregnated with fine abrasives.

lightly press the tool against the wheels to buff the leading and trailing faces of the cutting edge. This will create the sharpest possible edge.

There are several types of commercial buffing wheels to choose from — cloth, felt, leather, and rubber-bonded abrasive wheels. (SEE FIGURE 3-5.) The soft surfaces of these wheels tend to round the cutting edge the same way leather strops do. (SEE FIGURE 3-6.) You'll likely get the best results from the hardest wheel available. In fact, you can make a better buffing wheel than you can buy from hard *pressboard* — the same stuff that siding is made from. (SEE FIGURE 3-7.)

A SAFETY REMINDER

You cannot mount buffing wheels on a bench grinder because the wheels turn *toward* the cutting edge — the soft wheels will grab the tool and throw it at you. Nor can you mount grinding wheels on a buffing head — they aren't properly guarded. If you want a machine that can safely mount both grinding and buffing wheels, you have to build one — see page 95 for plans and instructions.

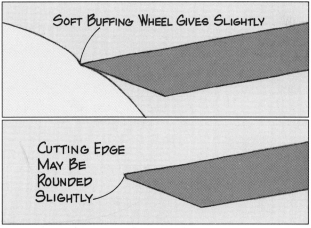

SOFT BUFFING WHEEL GIVES SLIGHTLY

CUTTING EDGE MAY BE ROUNDED SLIGHTLY

3-6 Most commercial buffing wheels have a soft surface that gives slightly as you hold a tool against it. This, in turn, may round over the cutting edge. To avoid this, press very lightly and don't hold the tool against the wheel for too long. The edge may still be slightly rounded, but the rounding shouldn't be pronounced enough to cause a problem.

3-7 You can make excellent
buffing wheels from *pressboard* —
the same material that siding is made
from. Purchase some pressboard siding or ask a contractor for a scrap,
then cut out 4-inch-diameter wheels
with a hole saw or band saw. Drill
1/2-inch-diameter arbor holes and
mount the wheels on your buffing
head. Rig a temporary tool rest and
true the wheels with a lathe chisel.
You can also turn the wheel edges
to different shapes (flat, round, or
pointed) to match the shapes of your
cutting edges. Load the wheels with
buffing compound.

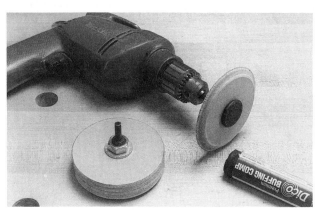

3-9 Small, shank-mounted
stropping wheels are used to buff
knives and carving tools. Like their
larger cousins, they must be used
with abrasive buffing compounds.

There are also dozens of *shank-mounted* grinding
wheels and strops, designed to be mounted in drills,
drill presses, and other rotary tools. (*SEE FIGURES 3-8 AND
3-9.*) These are essentially miniature dry grinders and
buffing wheels.

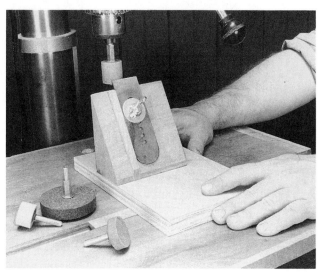

3-8 Shank-mounted grindstones
come in a variety of grits, shapes,
and sizes. They are designed to be
mounted in drills and other rotary
tools. By themselves, they will grind
tools to rough shape and touch up
cutting edges. To use them for precision sharpening tasks, you must
fashion tool rests or tool holders for
them. For example, the setup shown
holds a plane iron at a precise angle
to a small drum-shaped grindstone.

WET GRINDERS

Wet grinders, the second type of hollow grinder, bathe
their grinding wheels in water. (*SEE FIGURE 3-10.*) This
floats away the metal filings and keeps the work cool
as you grind it. They turn at a much slower speed (70
to 400 rpm) and have slightly larger wheels (10 inches)
than dry bench grinders. They hollow grind to a much
larger radius at the edge, and you can grind flat on the
sides, if you wish.

Unlike dry grinders, wet grinders allow you to hone
and polish. The larger grinding wheels are available
in grits up to 1,000, but only a few woodworking
tools benefit from an edge that's hollow ground right
to the tip. These include bench knives, carving
knives, and some small carving chisels. If you purchase a special side-grinding wheel, you can hone

and polish chisels, plane irons, and other cutting tools that require flat surfaces, but these stones are very expensive and there are other sharpening machines that will do this easier. (For an explanation of why hollow grinding is not suitable for many woodworking tools, refer to page 51.)

For Your Information

Advertisements for wet grinders often boast that these machines, by keeping the work cool, will not "draw the temper out" of a cutting edge. This is misleading. You cannot remove the temper from a cutting tool; it's *tempered* to reduce the hardness to the proper level after the tool is hardened. (See "Tool Steels and Carbides" on page 14.) A wet grinder helps keep the cutting edge cool so as not to further reduce the hardness of a tool.

3-10 Wet grinders bathe the grinding wheels in water to float away the swarf and keep the work cool. This particular machine combines a large wet wheel and a smaller dry wheel.

MOUNTING AND DRESSING GRINDING WHEELS

Grinding wheels require some maintenance. First of all, they are not always perfectly round when you buy them, and the arbors you mount them on may not run perfectly true. Furthermore, grinding wheels often become lopsided as they wear, the working surface accumulates grooves and chips, and the abrasive loads with metal filings. To mend out-of-round, worn, or loaded grinding wheels, you must dress the grinding surface.

1 **Before mounting and** dressing a grinding wheel, check it for cracks. Suspend the wheel on a length of wooden dowel, as shown, and strike it with a piece of hardwood. A good wheel will ring; a cracked wheel will sound dull. *Don't* remove the paper washers to check for cracks; these keep the large flange washers on the grinder from crushing the stone.

(continued) ▷

MOUNTING AND DRESSING GRINDING WHEELS — CONTINUED

2 **Mount the wheel on the** arbor, and be careful not to over-tighten the nut. The arbor is threaded in such a way that the rotation tightens the nut if it loosens. Replace all guards and shrouds, step aside, and turn on the machine. Let it run for a few minutes to be certain that the grinding wheel is solid and won't fly apart. Then, using a star-wheel dresser as shown, rough dress the wheel. This will round the wheel and expose fresh abrasive, but it will leave the surface too rough to use.

3 **Smooth the wheel surface** with a carbide stick or a diamond-point dresser. If you use a diamond-point dresser, make a simple holder, as shown. Keep the holder pressed firmly against the forward edge of the tool rest as you guide the dresser across the wheel. This will cut the grinding surface perfectly round and smooth. **Note:** You can also use dressing tools to shape the grinding surface, making it convex, concave, or pointed.

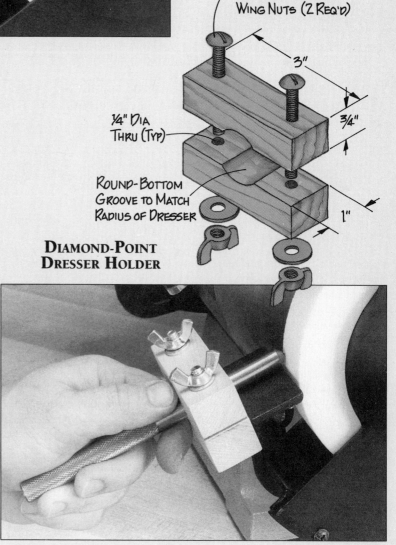

¼" x 2" RH MACHINE
SCREWS, WASHERS &
WING NUTS (2 REQ'D)

3"

¾"

¼" DIA
THRU (TYP)

ROUND-BOTTOM
GROOVE TO MATCH
RADIUS OF DRESSER

1"

**DIAMOND-POINT
DRESSER HOLDER**

FLAT GRINDERS

For most woodworkers, sharpening machines that grind a flat surface are more useful than hollow grinders. There are two types of flat grinders — motorized whetstones and abrasive belt sanders.

MOTORIZED WHETSTONES

A motorized whetstone also mounts a grinding wheel, but the wheel is held horizontally and the work is ground flat against the top surface of the wheel. There are two types — wet and dry — and the wheels may

spin anywhere from 400 rpm to 3,450 rpm. The better machines spin slowly. (SEE FIGURES 3-11 THROUGH 3-13.)

The horizontal grinding wheels can be changed easily, and they are available in many grits (from 100 to 1,200), so you can grind, hone, and polish on the same machine. The wheels are often *waterstones,* made of aluminum oxide abrasive in a soft clay binder. Water drips slowly onto the abrasive from a reservoir, and runs off into a trough. Some machines recycle this water; most don't, requiring you to fill the reservoir from time to time.

3-11 A *motorized whetstone* mounts a grinding wheel horizontally, allowing you to grind tools flat on the top surface. The machine may be wet or dry — the one shown is wet. Water drips from the reservoir onto the stone as it spins. The stones are easily changed and come in several grits, so you can grind, hone, and polish on the same machine.

3-12 You can purchase auxiliary tool rests for some motorized whetstones. This type of adjustable rest is much sturdier than the one that comes with the tool. With the tool clamped in the holder, it's easier to control the cutting edge as it's ground. The tool rest is often sold as a fixture for jointer and planer knives, but it's also useful for sharpening chisels and plane irons.

3-13 The commercial tool rests available for motorized whetstones are all designed to support tools with flat cutting edges. To sharpen a gouge, which has a curved edge, make a V-block support and attach it to the machine's rest. This will allow you to rotate or roll the tool as it's ground. The plans for this V-block can be found on page 57.

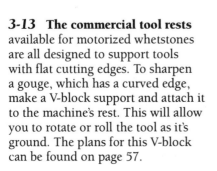

TRY THIS TRICK

Make your own low-cost abrasive wheels that can be used without water. Using the factory-supplied grinding wheel as a pattern, make several extra "wheels" from medium-density fiberboard (MDF). Cover the top surfaces with various grits of aluminum oxide and silicon-carbide sandpaper, sticking the sheets down with spray adhesive. When the sandpaper becomes worn or loaded, simply peel it up and stick down a fresh sheet. You can even make a hone by gluing ordinary typing paper to an MDF wheel, then applying buffing compound to the paper.

BELT SANDERS

Belt sanders, particularly 1- and 2-inch *strip sanders,* make excellent sharpening tools. *(SEE FIGURES 3-14 THROUGH 3-16.)* These machines grind flat surfaces, and a wide variety of abrasive belts are available (up to 600-grit). You can even mount leather belts, load the belts with buffing compounds, and use them as motorized strops.

However, you must pick the right sort of strip sander. Only a few are made specifically for sharpening. (These are sometimes referred to as *knife sharpeners.*) Most are designed for general woodworking, and you will have to modify them before you can use them to sharpen. Look for a *belt-driven* model with a 1,725-rpm reversible induction motor. Straight out of the box, the sander will probably run too fast and in the wrong direction — on most machines, the belt travels down past the table between 2,500 and 3,200 fpm. Change the pulleys so it runs less than 1,600 fpm. (For many tools, this can be done by using the same size pulleys on both the motor and the drive shaft.) Follow the directions on the motor label to reverse the rotation so the belt travels up past the table.

There are other considerations, too. The tables that come with most strip sanders aren't particularly useful as tool rests. They're too large and may not tilt as far as needed. You must either purchase an auxiliary tool rest or fashion one of your own. The tools you grind can be no wider than the belts, restricting the types of tools you can sharpen, especially on a 1-inch-wide strip sander.

3-14 You can use most stationary belt sanders to grind cutting tools. However, you cannot always use them to hone or polish since it's difficult to find wide sanding belts in grades finer than 150-grit.

3-15 This *knife sharpener* is a 1-inch strip sander that has been configured for sharpening knives and chisels. It will also mount a buffing wheel or drum. *Photo courtesy of Grizzly Imports, Inc.*

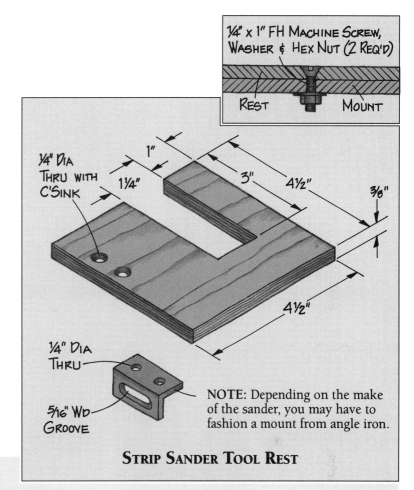

¼" x 1" FH Machine Screw, Washer & Hex Nut (2 Req'd)

REST   MOUNT

¼" Dia Thru with C'Sink

1"

1¼"

3"

4½"

3⁄8"

4½"

¼" Dia Thru

5⁄16" Wd Groove

NOTE: Depending on the make of the sander, you may have to fashion a mount from angle iron.

STRIP SANDER TOOL REST

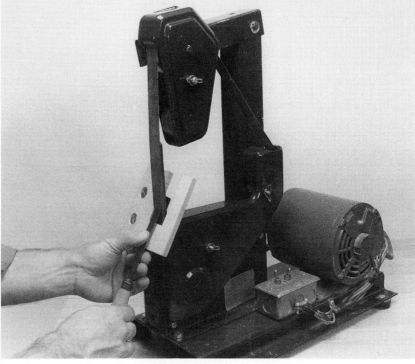

3-16 An ordinary *strip sander* is designed for woodworking and must be modified somewhat before it can be used as a sharpening machine. Change the pulleys and the motor rotation so the belt runs less than 1,600 fpm, traveling up as it passes the table. Also replace the table that comes with the sander with a tool rest. Shown is a small shop-made tool rest that works well for flat chisels. A more versatile rest is shown in the "Strip Sander Sharpening System" on page 107.

When you use the sander to sharpen, remember that the belts don't always run perfectly flat. They tend to cup in humid weather. This can be corrected with a little pressure, but if you don't catch it, a cupped belt could ruin your attempt to grind a straight edge. (SEE FIGURE 3-17.)

When choosing a sharpening machine, your overriding concern should be speed. *Slower is better* — on slow machines, the work does not heat as quickly and it's easier to control the amount of metal you remove. Also consider the available abrasive grades and the ease of changing grades.

WHERE TO FIND IT

Bench grinders, wet grinders, and motorized whetstones are sold through many mail-order woodworking suppliers, including:

Woodcraft
210 Wood County Industrial Park
P.O. Box 1686
Parkersburg, WV 26102

Strip sanders are sold by:

American Machine and Tool Company
Fourth Avenue and Spring Street
Royersford, PA 19468

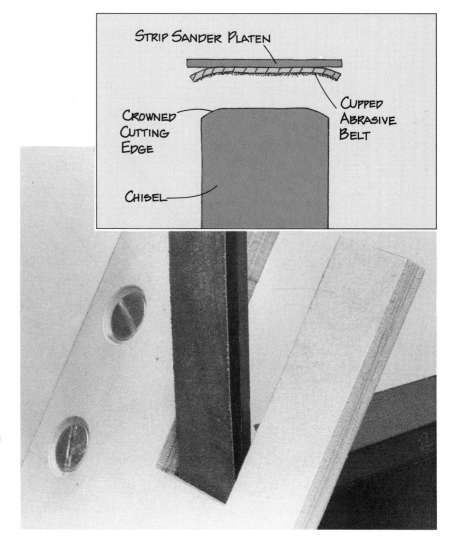

3-17 A sanding belt may cup slightly when it's mounted, especially when the weather is humid. When this happens, you must apply a little extra pressure as you sharpen — this will flatten the belt against the platen. If the pressure is too light, a cupped belt may remove more metal from the sides of the cutting edge than from the middle, making the edge crowned.

4

SHARPENING CHISELS AND PLANE IRONS

In some ways, sharpening tools is akin to finishing wood — everybody has a favorite technique. Ask five craftsmen how to sharpen a chisel, and you'll get five different recommendations of favorite materials, machines, and procedures. And if the craftsmen are reasonably savvy, all five techniques may work well.

There is no one best way to sharpen a chisel. Many sharpening recipes are effective, as long as they follow the three basic sharpening rules explained in the first chapter:

■ Restore the surfaces to the proper shape.

■ Maintain the proper tool geometry and hold that geometry throughout the procedure.

■ Finish the surfaces with progressively finer abrasives to create a keen edge.

The best sharpening technique *for you* is whichever one allows you to perform these tasks easily and accurately in a reasonable amount of time, using materials you feel comfortable with.

BASIC SHARPENING TECHNIQUES

The simplest tools to sharpen are those with the simplest surfaces — flat chisels and plane irons. The blade is just an elongated piece of tool steel with a beveled edge. The cutting edge is a straight, acute arris where the *bevel* meets the *back*. (SEE FIGURE 4-1.)

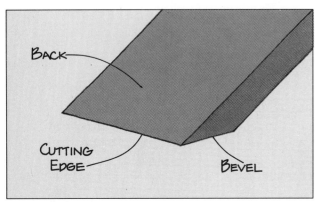

4-1 Flat chisels and plane irons are the simplest cutting tools — just elongated bars of steel with beveled edges. The cutting edge is where the *bevel* meets the *back*. These two surfaces are not the same size — the area of the back is much larger than that of the bevel. Consequently, it's easier to remove metal from the bevel than from the back. Initially, both surfaces must be ground, but after the first sharpening, most of the grinding, honing, polishing, and buffing takes place on the bevel.

GATHERING THE MATERIALS

The first step in any sharpening procedure is to gather the right abrasives for the job and make sure that they're in good condition. (SEE FIGURE 4-2.) As mentioned in previous chapters, there are four sharpening operations, and you'll need a different abrasive grade for each one:

■ *Coarse* abrasive (usually between 100- and 280-grit) to *grind* the surfaces, removing nicks and chips and restoring (or changing) the shape and geometry of the cutting edge

■ *Medium* abrasive (between 280- and 700-grit) to *hone,* removing the scratches left by grinding and drawing the cutting edge out to a sharp point

■ *Fine* abrasive (between 700- and 1,200-grit) to *polish* the surfaces and create a keen cutting edge

■ *Extra-fine* abrasive (1,200-grit or finer) to *buff* the surfaces to a mirror finish and draw the cutting edge to the sharpest possible point

This isn't to imply that you always need four different abrasives to sharpen a tool. Depending on the quality of the steel in a tool and how the tool is used, it's often not worth the effort to polish or buff the surfaces. Many turners, for example, only grind and hone the chisels they use to rough out a shape on the lathe. Or, if the surfaces of a cutting tool are in fairly good shape and the edge isn't rounded, you may be able to skip the grinding and just hone, polish, or buff. Many craftsmen frequently *touch up* tool edges as they work by rubbing them across a fine stone or a strop to keep them razor sharp.

4-2 Here are the basic tools and materials needed to hand sharpen a very dull flat chisel with natural Arkansas abrasives: A *coarse washita stone* (1), a *medium-soft Arkansas stone* (2), a *fine hard black Arkansas stone* (3), *mineral oil* (4) to keep the stone clean, *rags* (5) to wipe away the oil, and a bright *light* (6) to inspect the cutting edge. You also might include a *strop* (7) and *buffing compound* (8) to create a super-keen edge, a *honing guide* (9) to maintain the proper tool angle and shape, and a *magnifying glass* (10) to inspect the edge close up.

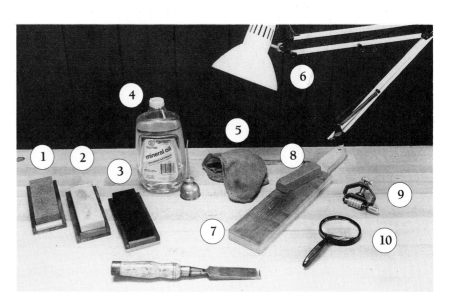

Make sure the stones you choose are clean and flat. If you use a sharpening machine, check that the abrasives are in good shape. If the stones must be used with liquids, or if you're using a wet grinder, have the necessary cleaner/coolant on hand. You'll also want a few rags to wipe the liquid off the tool.

One of the most important sharpening tools — and the most often overlooked — is a *bright light,* such as a tension lamp. You want to inspect the tool's surfaces as you sharpen them. If these surfaces are very small, you may also need a magnifying glass.

A SAFETY REMINDER

If you use a sharpening machine, wear safety glasses or a face shield to protect your eyes from abrasive grit and metal filings.

FLATTENING THE BACK

The first time you sharpen a chisel or a plane iron, *flatten* the back. Grind and hone the back on a perfectly flat stone or sharpener, pressing it gently against the abrasive. If you plan to polish or buff the bevel, polish and buff the back, too. (*SEE FIGURES 4-3 AND 4-4.*) Thereafter, you only need to touch up the back.

SETUP

If you're using a tool rest or a honing guide, set it to grind the proper angle. This angle depends on the type of tool and how it's used. Most flat chisels are sharpened at 30 degrees and most plane irons at 25 degrees. Light-duty tools and tools that are used to cut softwood can be sharpened at *slightly* smaller angles; heavy-duty tools and tools that cut hardwood may require *slightly* larger angles. If a chisel is hit with a mallet, it will require larger angles than one that is used with hand pressure. Many experienced craftsmen don't even measure the angles — they just know how *long* the bevel should appear, indicating that the precise angle on *hand tools* isn't critical.

There are two procedures for setting the angle of a honing guide or tool rest, depending on whether you want to change the tool angle or maintain it. To change the angle, mount the tool in the guide or rest and measure the angle between the back of the tool and

4-3 Flatten the back of a chisel or a plane iron on a bench stone, keeping the back against the abrasive surface as you rub it back and forth. Check your progress from time to time by inspecting the scratch pattern on the back. You know the back is flat when the scratch pattern covers the entire surface. Work your way through the abrasive grades, finishing the back to the same degree that you plan to finish the bevel.

4-4 You can also flatten the back of flat chisels and plane irons on motorized whetstones. To flatten a chisel, remove the tool rest and lay the chisel flat on the spinning stone as you hold it by its handle. To flatten a plane iron, mount it to a push block with double-faced carpet tape, then use the push block to keep the iron on the stone. In both cases, start with medium or even fine abrasives. Coarse abrasives may remove metal from the back too quickly.

the abrasive surface. (SEE FIGURE 4-5.) Adjust the guide or rest until the angle is correct. If you want to maintain the angle, simply set up the guide or the rest so the bevel lays flat against the abrasive. Make a few swipes across the abrasive to check that it contacts the entire surface, not just the heel or tip of the bevel. (SEE FIGURE 4-6.)

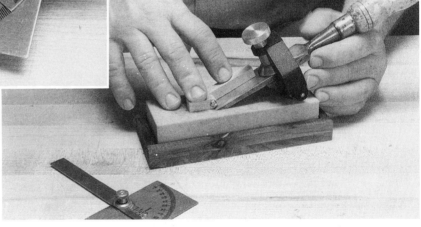

4-5 One of the simplest ways to measure the tool angle when you set up a honing guide or a tool rest is to use a magnetic protractor, as shown on page 31. If you don't have one of these, the next best thing is to copy the angle with a small shop-made L-bevel (shown), then measure the angle with an ordinary protractor.

4-6 You may not need to measure the tool angle at all if you want to maintain the current angle. Simply set up the honing guide and make a few swipes across the bench stone. If

you're using a sharpening machine with a tool rest, turn on the machine for a second and touch the tool to the abrasive. Inspect the bevel — if just the tip is scratched (*left*), the

tool angle is too large. If just the heel is scratched (*middle*), the tool angle is too small. If the entire surface of the bevel is scratched (*right*), the angle is right on the money.

As mentioned in previous chapters, I highly recommend using a honing guide or a tool holder of some sort to maintain the precise angle of the bevel, especially when grinding and honing substantial amounts of metal from the tool. This prevents inadvertently rocking the tool and rounding the bevel. As explained on page 6, rounding the bevel increases the tool angle at the expense of the clearance and cutting angles.

However, setting up a guide or a rest can be a nuisance when all you're doing is touching up a cutting edge. And it's not as necessary since you're removing only a little metal.

When you don't use a device to maintain the tool angle, *feel* the angle against the stone. (*SEE FIGURE 4-7.*) This is easier to do with a bench stone than with a sharpening machine for the simple reason that you can safely put your fingers closer to the bevel when hand sharpening. With a sharpening machine, you must keep your hands out of harm's way and *eyeball* the angle. (*SEE FIGURE 4-8.*) Before adjusting the tool stand, rest the cutting tool on it and pivot the stand this way and that until the angle looks right.

GRINDING, HONING, POLISHING, AND BUFFING

You must finish both the bevels *and* the backs of chisels and plane irons to create the sharpest possible edge. If you're using a honing guide to help grind the bevel, sharpen the back without removing the guide. If your sharpening the bevel on a machine, finish the back on bench stones. No matter what technique you use, remember to grind away almost all of the metal from the bevel — just touch up the back. Removing too much metal from the back will reduce the strength of the blade. (*SEE FIGURE 4-9.*)

When sharpening by hand, rub the tool across the abrasive so the cutting edge is perpendicular to the direction in which you're moving the tool. When sharpening on a machine, hold the tool so the edge is perpendicular to the direction the abrasive is traveling. (*SEE FIGURE 4-10.*) Either way, the abrasive should rub the tool so the scratches in the surface are roughly perpendicular to the edge. This will make the edge stronger and sharper.

When touching up a slightly worn cutting edge, just polish or buff the tool with the appropriate abrasive. If the tool is fairly dull, but the cutting edge isn't nicked,

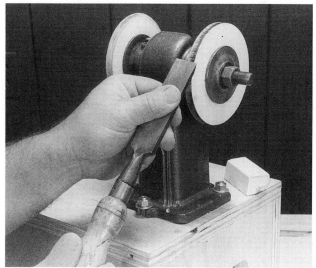

4-8 You can use a sharpening machine without setting the tool rest — just *eyeball* the angle. However, to be safe, don't forsake the rest entirely. Use it for support when you touch the tool to the abrasive, but pivot the tool on the rest to get the angle you want. Use this technique only when polishing or touching up a tool with *fine* abrasives. That way, you won't remove much metal if you misjudge the angle. Some craftsmen eyeball angles on a sharpening machine *only* when buffing with extra-fine compounds — this further limits the amount of metal that can be removed.

4-7 When hand sharpening or touching up tools without a honing guide, hold the tool with one or two fingers against the back and just above the bevel. Rock the tool until you feel the bevel resting flat against the stone. Carefully maintain this angle as you rub the tool back and forth across the stone.

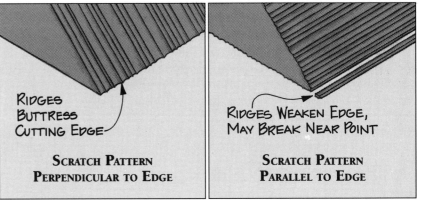

4-9 When sharpening flat chisels and plane irons, you must grind the back flat *initially*, but thereafter remove most of the metal from the bevel. If you continue to grind away metal from both the bevel and the back every time you sharpen the tool, the blade will become thinner and weaker.

4-10 A sharpening abrasive, no matter how fine, leaves a *scratch pattern* — microscopic ridges and valleys — in the metal surfaces of the tool. This pattern should be roughly perpendicular to the cutting edge. The ridges will buttress the cutting edge, making it stronger. There will also be less friction when you cut since the ridges are more or less aligned with the path of the cut. If the ridges are parallel to the cutting edge, the edge will be weak, generating more friction.

chipped, or visibly rounded, begin by honing, then polish and buff as needed. Only if the tool is badly worn, damaged, or incorrectly sharpened should you need to start grinding away the surfaces with coarse abrasives.

cutting edge. You'll save time and extend the life of the blade by doing all the heavy work with coarse abrasives, moving to finer abrasives only after the tool has been ground to the desired shape and geometry.

FOR BEST RESULTS

Never hand grind a tool with an abrasive coarser than 100-grit or machine grind with abrasive coarser than 60-grit. Extremely coarse abrasives remove metal too quickly to control. They also leave deep scratches in the leading and trailing faces that are difficult to remove when honing.

TRY THIS TRICK

Inspect the surface you're sharpening to tell if it's time to change abrasive grades. When the metal surface is an even color and texture, with no dull areas, shiny spots, or scratch lines, change to a finer grit.

However, one of the most common sharpening mistakes is starting out with an abrasive that's not coarse enough. Novices sometimes use medium or fine grits to remove nicks and chips, flatten surfaces, and even change the bevel angle. If you're sharpening by hand, this will cost you lots of extra work. And if you're sharpening on a machine, these grits will not only take longer but also may generate enough heat to burn the

Note: When you inadvertently overheat a tool during sharpening and the surface turns blue or purple, don't automatically think that you've ruined the tool. The damage that you've done depends on the type of steel and how far the color has traveled along the metal. Good tool steel may soften slightly — its ability to take and hold a sharp edge may be reduced — but only the discolored portion is damaged. If the color hasn't traveled too far, just grind down past it, being careful not to overheat the tool again. High-speed steel

4-11 As you sharpen, take care to preserve the profile of the blade. Usually, the cutting edge should be straight and perpendicular to the blade side. Using a small square, check the profile from time to time as you sharpen.

may not soften at all — you often have to draw a red or straw color before you reduce the hardness of this material. If the sharpening machine overheats the work frequently and you're using the proper grade of abrasive, the machine is running too fast or you're using too much pressure.

As you sharpen, you must grind not only the correct tool angle and shape of the faces but also the profile of the tool itself. If the cutting edge is supposed to be square to the side of the blade, then grind it that way. (*See Figure 4-11.*) If the cutting edge is supposed to be straight across, prevent it from becoming crowned or dished as you work. (*See Figure 4-12.*) If the profile is slightly out of kilter, fix it by applying a little pressure to one side of the blade or the other as you sharpen. (*See Figure 4-13.*)

If you have trouble correcting the profile, or the profile grows more misshapen, then several things could be wrong. Most likely, you've mounted the tool in the honing guide at a slight angle or you're holding it slightly skewed on the tool rest — check your setup. If the setup is correct, check that the surface of the abrasive is flat. If not, dress the abrasive as shown on page 24.

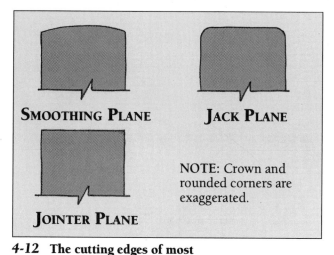

SMOOTHING PLANE   **JACK PLANE**

JOINTER PLANE

NOTE: Crown and rounded corners are exaggerated.

4-12 The cutting edges of most flat chisels are ground straight, but this is not necessarily so with plane irons. You can grind a gentle crown in the edge of smoothing plane irons to allow you to cut a little deeper and remove stock faster. You can also slightly round the corners of jack plane irons to prevent them from leaving ridges as they cut. Jointer plane irons, of course, should always be ground perfectly straight and square in order to cut a perfectly flat surface.

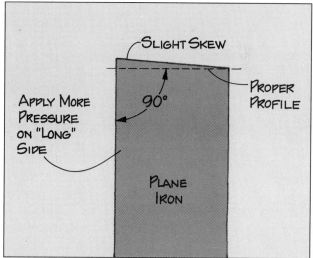

SLIGHT SKEW

PROPER PROFILE

APPLY MORE PRESSURE ON "LONG" SIDE

90°

PLANE IRON

4-13 If you inadvertently grind a chisel or a plane iron to the wrong profile, you can easily correct it with some extra grinding and a judicious application of pressure. In the example shown, you should apply a little extra sharpening pressure to the *long* side of the cutting edge, grinding it back so it's perpendicular to the blade side. If you have trouble correcting the profile, check your setup and the surface of the abrasive.

TRY THIS TRICK

To help maintain the correct profile, mark a reference line on the back of the blade, near the cutting edge, with a fine china marker. Grind the cutting edge parallel to the reference line.

As the edge becomes sharper, a burr (also called a *wire edge*) will roll up on the back — you can feel it with the tip of your finger. Ignore the burr until you've finished sharpening the bevel. Then turn the tool over and rub the back across the last abrasive used a few times to remove the burr. (SEE FIGURE 4-14.) Inspect the edge under bright light — vestiges of the burr and any remaining defects will reflect the light, showing up as bright spots. If the edge reflects no light, test it by cutting across the grain of a scrap of wood. (SEE FIGURE 4-15.)

A SAFETY REMINDER

You can't tell as much about an edge by running your finger across it as you can by inspecting it under a bright light or by cutting across wood grain. However, if you insist on performing this traditional ritual, be sure to run your finger *across* the cutting edge (perpendicular to it) and not *along* it (parallel to the sharp arris). If you sharpen a tool correctly and then run your finger along the edge, you'll wish you weren't such a traditionalist.

4-14 When you've finished sharpening the bevel, you must remove the burr that forms on the back. Turn the tool over and rub it across the last abrasive used several times. Don't remove the honing guide or change the angle of the tool rest yet. To remove the last vestiges of the burr, it sometimes helps to take a few additional licks on the last stone or the strop, alternating between the bevel and the back.

4-15 Test the sharpness of the finished edge by cutting a thin slice *across* the grain of a scrap of wood, near the end. If the edge isn't sharp enough, this cut will require a lot of force. Any remaining defects in the edge — microscopic nicks or traces of the burr — can be detected by tiny lines of torn fibers in the cut surface.

Microbevels and Hollow Bevels

MICROSHARPENING

Many craftsmen prefer to add a *microbevel* to a cutting edge after they polish it. *(See Figure 4-16.)* A microbevel (also called a *secondary bevel*) is a tiny bevel right at the point of the cutting edge that increases the bevel angle. This makes the edge more durable. (It does *not*, by the way, make the edge sharper — that's a myth.) But because the microbevel is so small, the force required to make the cut increases only slightly, sometimes imperceptibly.

To make a microbevel, adjust the honing guide or the tool holder to increase the tool angle. If the tool angle that you use to sharpen is extremely acute — 15 to 20 degrees — increase it by 5 to 7 degrees. If the tool angle is less acute — 25 degrees or more — increase it by 3 to 5 degrees. Then rub the cutting edge across the finest stone, making no more than two or three passes.

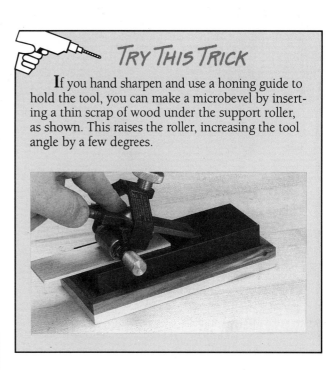

Try This Trick

If you hand sharpen and use a honing guide to hold the tool, you can make a microbevel by inserting a thin scrap of wood under the support roller, as shown. This raises the roller, increasing the tool angle by a few degrees.

4-16 A microbevel is a microscopic secondary bevel at the cutting edge that increases the bevel angle by a few degrees. To make a microbevel, rub the cutting edge across a fine stone two or three times, no more. You can add this microbevel to either the back or the face of the tool, as shown.

Although this sounds like a good idea, think twice before you decide to make a microbevel. First of all, it's doubtful whether cutting tools with large tool angles (30 degrees or more) need a microbevel. And when you increase the tool angle, you decrease one of the other two. Depending on how the tool is positioned when it cuts, a microbevel will alter either the cutting angle or the clearance angle. If the cutting angle is critical, or the clearance angle is very small, this could adversely affect the way the tool cuts.

When the cutting angle is critical, make the microbevel in the trailing face, where it will affect the clearance angle. When the clearance angle is extremely small, put the microbevel in the leading face so it decreases the cutting angle. *(See Figure 4-17.)* When the cutting angle is critical *and* the clearance angle is small, forget the microbevel.

HOLLOW GRINDING

You can hollow grind the bevel of certain *light-duty* woodworking tools, such as carving knives and chisels. This decreases the tool angle so the tool cuts more smoothly with less effort, even though the edge is less durable. But since the tool isn't used heavily, the edge doesn't dull too quickly and the trade-off is acceptable.

However, *don't* use this sharpening technique for anything other than light-duty tools. When you hollow

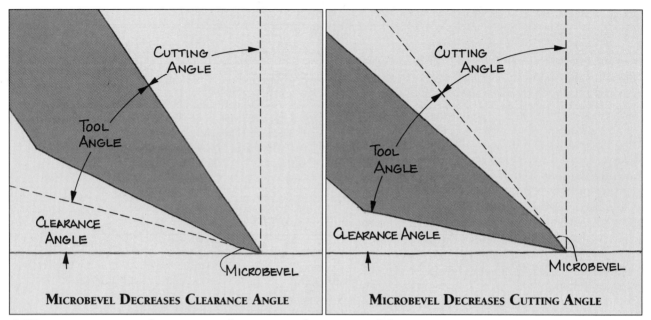

MICROBEVEL DECREASES CLEARANCE ANGLE

MICROBEVEL DECREASES CUTTING ANGLE

4-17 In most cases, it's best to make a microbevel in the trailing face of the tool so it decreases the clearance angle, as shown on the left. This is because the clearance angle is usually less critical than the cutting angle. However, if the clearance angle is extremely small, you will be better off making the microbevel in the leading face, as shown on the right.

grind a bevel, the tool angle at the tip is a great deal less than the apparent grinding angle, and this weakens the cutting edge. Depending on the tool and how it's used, the edge may chip or even snap off. You can adjust the grinding angle to make a higher tool angle, but the clearance angle disappears. The heel of the bevel may prevent the cutting edge from contacting the wood when the tool is held at the proper cutting angle. (*See Figure 4-18.*)

You can, however, hollow grind the bevel of a medium-duty cutting edge *before* sharpening a tool by grinding the bevel concave, then honing the tip flat. The purpose of this technique is two-fold: It cuts down on the sharpening time and increases the clearance on the back surface.

When the bevel is flat, you have to grind, hone, and polish the entire surface. This isn't a big consideration if you sharpen your tools on a machine, but it can be

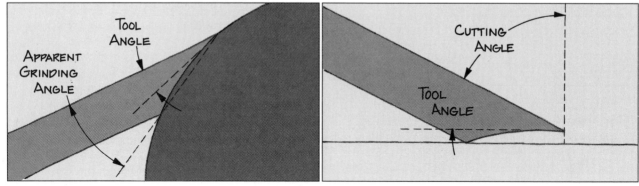

4-18 There are two good reasons *not* to hollow grind medium-duty and heavy-duty cutting tools. First, it decreases the tool angle and weakens the cutting edge. Second, if you adjust the grind to make the tip less fragile, then the clearance angle disappears.

time consuming when you sharpen them by hand. When the bevel is hollow ground, you only have to sharpen the tip. Because you're removing less metal, the time required to sharpen the edge decreases. (*SEE FIGURE 4-19.*)

Note: Many craftsmen prefer to sharpen a hollow bevel so both the tip *and* the heel are ground flat. This makes it easier to feel the angle when you touch up the edge of a tool without a honing guide or a tool rest.

The hollowed-out bevel also helps the back of the tool to clear the wood. It doesn't increase the clearance angle at the cutting edge, of course. Because the

tip is ground flat, this angle remains the same as on an ordinary flat-ground tool. But there is more room at the back, which can be useful.

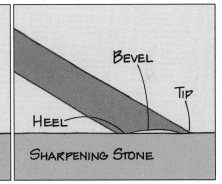

FOR BEST RESULTS

The smaller the radius of the grindstone that you use to hollow grind, the more metal is removed from the bevel and the weaker the tool grows. For this reason, use the largest available grindstone for hollow grinding.

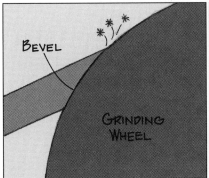

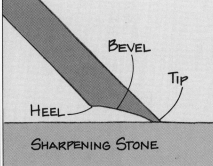

4-19 To reduce the time and effort required to sharpen a tool, hollow grind the bevel on a bench grinder or wet grinder, as shown on the left. When you sharpen the concave bevel on a flat stone, adjust the

angle so just the tip of the bevel contacts the stone, as shown in the middle. Or if you prefer, adjust the angle so the tip *and* the heel make contact, as shown on the right. Either way, you'll remove less metal, and the

sharpening process will go faster. You can usually resharpen a tool several times before the flat areas expand and it needs to be hollow ground again.

FINE TUNING A HAND PLANE

Once you sharpen the blade, good-quality hand planes usually work fairly well just as they come from the manufacturer. However, even the best can benefit from judicious tuning. Old-timers refer to this as *fettling* a hand plane.

1 **Sharpen your plane iron,** making sure the back is perfectly flat. Check that the plane iron rests solidly on the frog, or the supporting surface. If the iron rocks, file the support flat. Be careful when you do this. Often all that's needed is one or two strokes of the file to remove a tiny burr.

(continued) ▷

FINE TUNING A HAND PLANE — CONTINUED

2 **A plane will only cut as true** as its sole. Check the flatness of the sole by resting it on a perfectly flat surface such as a jointer table. If you can see any daylight between the sole and the table, grind the sole flat. Affix wet/dry sandpaper to a large ¼-inch-thick plate of glass with contact cement. Using water to float away the metal filings, rub the plane back and forth until the sole is uniformly gray. (A shiny spot indicates an area of the sole that is still low.) Start with 120-grit paper and finish with 320-grit. Some craftsmen prefer to work their way up to 600-grit or higher for an ultrasmooth sole. **Note:** Remove

the iron, but leave the frog (if there is one) attached when you grind the sole flat. Otherwise, the sole may be stressed and pulled out of true when you tighten the screws that hold the frog in place.

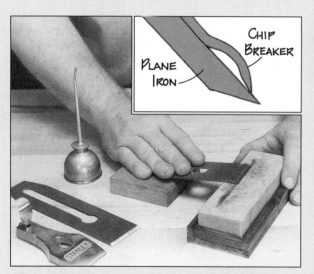

3 **The edge of the chip breaker** should contact the entire width of the plane iron with no visible gaps. If the chip breaker doesn't fit correctly after you flatten the back of the iron, grind the edge straight on a sharpening stone, as shown. Note that the body of the chip breaker is off the stone and *lower* than the edge that's being ground — this creates the proper angle. You will ruin the chip breaker if you grind it with the body on the stone.

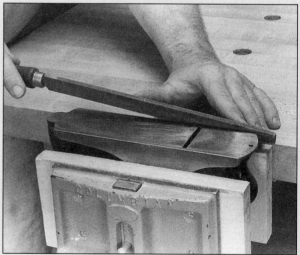

4 **Remove all the burrs and** imperfections from the cast metal parts. *Lightly* file the surface of the cam in the lever cap to make it smooth, and clean up the edges of the mouth, if necessary. Most important, file a tiny chamfer all around the perimeter of the sole. This will keep the edge of the sole from digging into the wood.

5

SHARPENING GOUGES, KNIVES, AND SCRAPERS

Many techniques used to sharpen flat chisels and plane irons can be used with cutting tools such as skew chisels, gouges, V-tools, knives, and even scrapers. However, the cutting edges of these hand tools are more complex and require special materials and techniques for sharpening. Skew chisels, for example, are ground at compound angles. Gouges and V-tools have curved or V-shaped blades. The cutting edge of a knife is crowned and runs along the side of the blade instead of the tip. A scraper has no visible cutting edge, just a microscopic burr.

SHARPENING SKEW CHISELS, GOUGES, AND V-TOOLS

Because the blades of skews, gouges, and V-tools are more complex in shape than those of flat chisels and plane irons, it's more difficult to grind them. (*SEE FIGURE 5-1.*) You must devise some method of holding these blades at the proper angle to the stone or the abrasive.

When working on a sharpening machine, you can easily create specially shaped guide blocks for all but the most complex tools and attach them to the tool rest. Use an angled block for skew chisels — set the bevel by tilting the tool rest, and create the skew by guiding the chisel along the angled side. (*SEE FIGURES 5-2 AND 5-3.*) Make a V-block for gouges, and keep the blade pressed against the sides of the V as you rotate the cutting edge. (*SEE FIGURE 5-4.*) Use a trapezoid block for V-tools, and guide the blade along the angled sides when grinding the two separate cutting edges. (*SEE FIGURE 5-5.*)

5-1 When sharpening cutting edges with complex shapes, you face the same problem as when sharpening ordinary chisels and plane irons — how do you hold them at the proper angle to the abrasive as you grind? A *skew chisel* (1) must be held at a complex angle to grind the bevel *and* the skew. A *gouge* (2) must be rolled from side to side as it's ground to follow the curve of the cutting edge. And both sides of a *V-tool* (3) must be ground precisely the same.

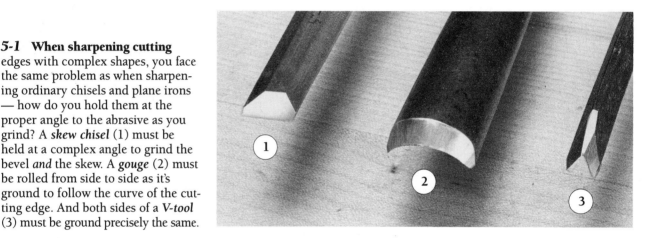

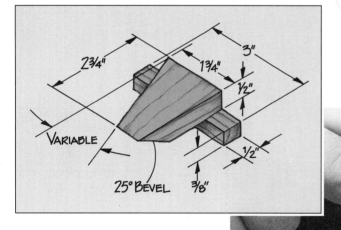

5-2 When machine sharpening a skew chisel with a single bevel, make a guide block with one angled side, as shown. Clamp this to the tool rest. Hold the side of the chisel against the angled side as you grind the bevel. The angle of the tool rest controls the bevel angle, and the angled side of the block controls the skew angle.

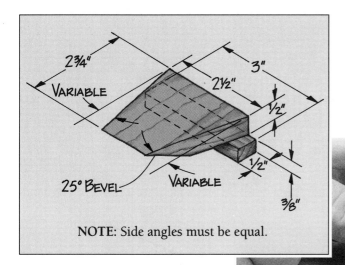

NOTE: Side angles must be equal.

5-3 When machine sharpening a skew chisel with a double bevel (such as a lathe skew), make a guide block in the shape of a trapezoid with two equal sides and angles. Hold the skew against one of the equal sides when grinding one bevel, then turn it over and hold it against the other equal side to grind the second bevel.

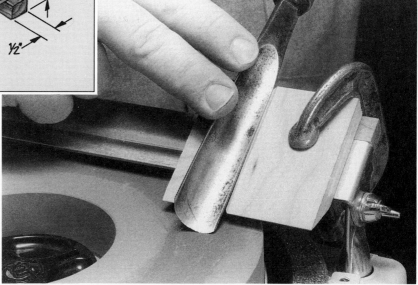

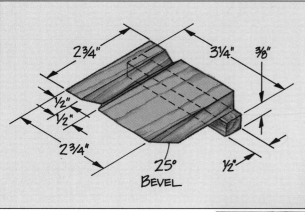

5-4 To grind the curved edge of a gouge, make a guide block with a V-groove, as shown. Rest the blade of the gouge in the V and hold it there as you roll the tool. Press the tool forward gently to keep the cutting edge against the abrasive as the gouge rolls.

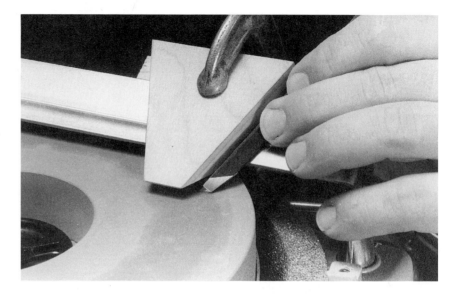

5-5 Sharpening a V-tool is like sharpening two flat chisels joined at the sides. To do this, make a trapezoid guide block with *gently* angled sides, similar to the block used to sharpen double-bevel skews. Use the angled sides to guide the blade when grinding the bevels, keeping the top of each side of the tool against the block. The angles will give each bevel a slight skew, so the *ears* of the V-tool (the corners) will protrude slightly ahead of the *nose* (where the sides are joined). The reasoning behind this profile is explained in *Figure 5-15.*

5-6 When hand sharpening a complex edge, you often have to feel the angle. To feel it when sharpening skews and V-tools, try using a small slip stone. Press the slip stone against the bevel with your fingertips, as shown.

When hand sharpening, many craftsmen resort to feeling the tool angle. To do this, use small stones, such as slip stones or gouge slips, and hold them in your hand. (*See Figures 5-6 and 5-7.*) This makes it easier to sense the correct angle with your fingertips.

However, commercial honing guides are available for tools with complex cutting edges. (*See Figures 5-8 and 5-9.*) Or, you can make your own, as shown in "Sharpening Guides for Gouges and Knives" on page 67. These guides hold the cutting tool at the proper angle, yet allow you to roll or rotate the blade as needed. You can sharpen the complex edges of skews, gouges, and V-tools, as well as the simpler edges of ordinary flat chisels, with equal precision.

In addition to the fixtures and techniques needed to maintain the tool angle of a complex edge, there are other considerations:

■ *Skew chisels* — When sharpening a *double-faced* skew chisel, there are two bevels but no back. You must grind both bevels to the same angle and remove an equal amount of metal from each. (*See Figure 5-10.*)

■ *Gouges* — The concave back of a gouge must be ground, honed, and polished, just like the flat back on an ordinary chisel. To do this, use a slip stone or a gouge slip, or wrap a sheet of sandpaper around a dowel. (*See Figure 5-11.*) When grinding a turning gouge, you may elect to cut back the *ears* (the corners of the curved cutting edge), making the profile of the tool appear crowned. (*See Figure 5-12.*)

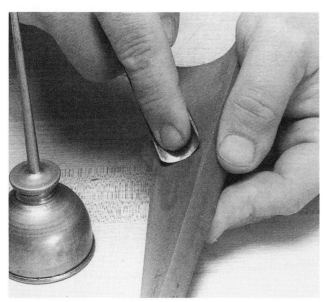

5-7 Use a gouge slip when hand sharpening a gouge. Put your fingertips on the concave back of the gouge to help feel the angle.

5-8 This clever honing guide clamps to the blade of a chisel and holds it at a precise angle to a bench stone, yet it allows you to rotate the blade to any angle. When sharpening a skew or a V-tool (shown), set the tool angle by adjusting the angle of the blade to the stone's surface. Then rotate the blade until the bevel rests flat on the stone, and lock the blade in place.

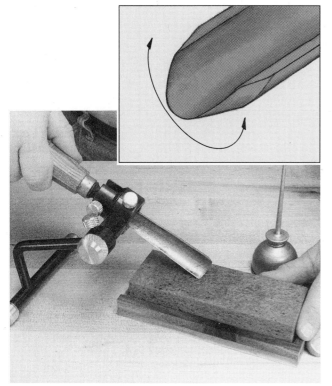

5-9 Sharpening a gouge is similar to sharpening a V-tool, but you don't lock the blade at any particular skew angle. Leave it unlocked so you can roll the blade as you move it back and forth across the abrasive.

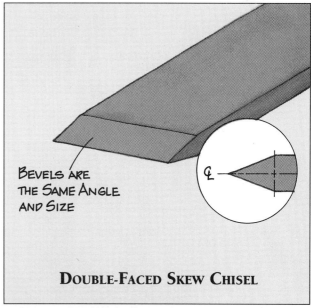

BEVELS ARE THE SAME ANGLE AND SIZE

DOUBLE-FACED SKEW CHISEL

5-10 A lathe skew has two bevels, each of which must be a mirror image of the other. Grind them to the same angle and the same length.

5-11   To sharpen the concave back of a gouge, find a stone or another tool with a curved surface that approximates its radius. Here, an ordinary hardwood dowel that has been coated with buffing compound is used to polish the back.

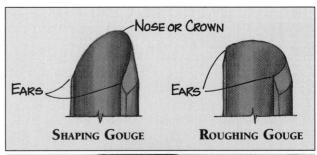

5-12   Turners often grind back the ears on gouges they use to shape spindles and bowls. This lets them cut concave shapes, called *coves*. If the bevel of the gouge is ground for shearing, the tool is often referred to as a *spindle gouge*. If it's ground for scraping, it is called a *bowl gouge*. Both fall under the heading of *shaping gouges*. Turners may also leave the ears on a gouge and use them to cut. This sort of turning gouge — called a *roughing gouge* — is often used to round blanks.

TRY THIS TRICK

After grinding, honing, and polishing a gouge, put a microbevel in the concave *back* with two or three strokes on an ultrafine round stone file, as shown. This not only creates a microbevel but also removes the burr. This trick also works for V-tools.

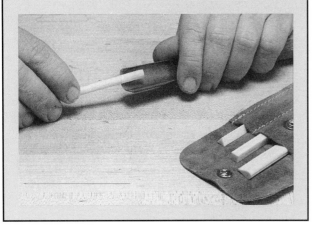

■ *V-tools* — Treat a V-tool as if it were two flat chisels joined at the side. Each bevel must be ground to precisely the same angle, and you must remove the same amount of stock from both. (SEE FIGURE 5-13.) After you grind the bevels flat, grind the *nose* (the point of the V) to same angle as the bevels. Some craftsmen prefer to slightly round the nose, grinding at the same angle as the bevel. Both techniques remove the small protrusion or *hook* that forms there. (SEE FIGURE 5-14.)

You may also wish to change the profile of the V-tool, as viewed from the side. Almost all V-tools come from the manufacturer ground with the nose a few degrees ahead of the ears. However, the tool will cut with much less effort if the ears are even with or slightly ahead of the nose. (SEE FIGURE 5-15.)

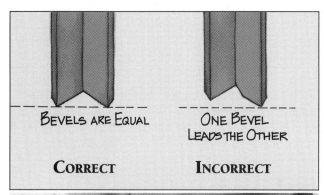

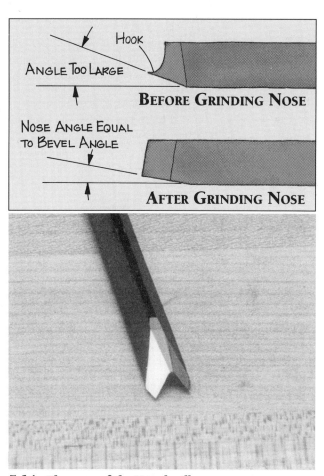

5-13 When grinding a V-tool, make sure both bevels are ground to the same angle and the same length. Also, be careful not to grind the bevels unevenly or one will protrude slightly.

5-14 The nose of the V-tool will develop a slight protrusion, called a *hook,* as you grind the bevels. Remove the hook by grinding the point of the V (where the bevels join) to the same angle as the bevels. Be careful not to grind too much; remove just enough metal to eliminate the hook.

5-15 As they come from the manufacturer, many V-tools are ground with the nose slightly ahead of the ears. The trouble with this arrangement is that the nose cuts the wood and begins to lift the chip before the ears have a chance to cut the sides of the groove. It makes more sense to let the ears lead the nose so the tool cuts the sides of the groove first, then cleans out the bottom.

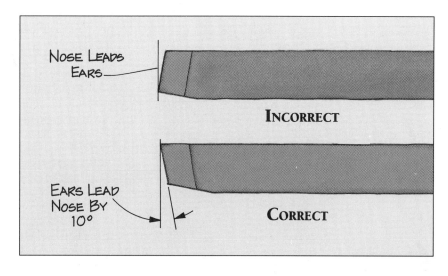

SHARPENING LATHE CHISELS

When you turn a spindle on a lathe, there are two ways to cut the wood. You can *shear,* using an extremely high cutting angle, or you can *scrape,* using a much lower cutting angle. The optimum tool angles are very different, too, but lathe tool manufacturers usually compromise when they grind their chisels. They sharpen them at an angle of 45 degrees, which supposedly makes it possible to scrape and shear with the same set of tools. The trouble is, this bastard angle won't do a great job of scraping or shearing. This has given rise to two misconceptions: Shearing is a difficult technique, and scraping produces a rough surface. Actually, both cutting techniques are relatively easy and both produce a smooth surface *if you grind your tools to the proper angles!*

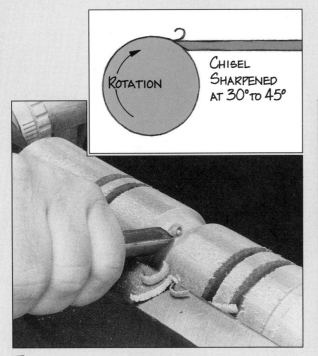

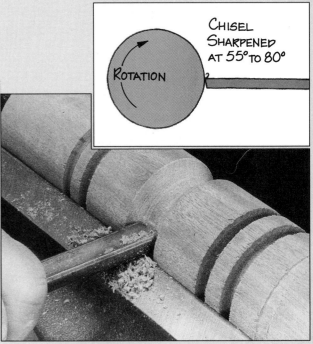

1   **When shearing on a lathe,** you cut with the chisel tangent to the circumference of the spindle, so the tool meets the wood at a high cutting angle. Because of this, the tool angle must be fairly low — 30 to 45 degrees. The chips roll off the chisel in long curls, and the surface of the wood appears to be planed smooth.

2   **To scrape on a lathe, you** must cut with the chisel pointed at the center of the spindle, using a low cutting angle. Because this cutting technique tends to compress the chip more than it lifts it, there's a lot of wear and tear at the cutting edge. The tool angle must be as high as possible to make it more durable — 55 to 80 degrees, which is similar to a cabinet scraper. Furthermore, you must take a very shallow cut. You cannot remove stock as quickly as when shearing, but if the tool is properly sharpened, the scraped surface will be almost as smooth.

3 **Because the sharpening** requirements for each cutting technique are so different, it's best not to scrape and shear with the same tools. Instead, invest in two sets of the lathe tools you use most often. Sharpen one set for shearing and the other for scraping, as shown in the chart "Tool Angles for Shearing and Scraping" below. As for the chisels that you don't duplicate, think about whether you use them mostly to scrape or to shear, then grind them to the appropriate angle. To easily tell the difference between your scraping and shearing tools, code the handles by color or stain the handles of one set dark.

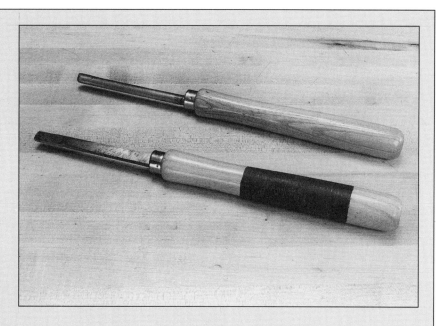

TOOL ANGLES FOR SHEARING AND SCRAPING

	SKEW CHISEL	ROUGHING GOUGE	SHAPING GOUGE	FLATNOSE CHISEL	ROUNDNOSE CHISEL	PARTING TOOL
PROFILES						
TOOL ANGLES FOR SHEARING	30°–35°	30°–35°	30°–35°	35°–40°	35°–40°	40°–45°
TOOL ANGLES FOR SCRAPING	75°–80°	55°–65°	55°–65°	75°–80°	75°–80°	75°–80°

SHARPENING KNIVES

Although a knife is perhaps the simplest of cutting tools, it can be deceptively complex to sharpen. The cutting edge is ground along the side of the blade rather than along the tip, and the profile of this edge is often curved or crowned. (SEE FIGURE 5-16.) These two characteristics combine to make it difficult to maintain an accurate and consistent tool angle when grinding, honing, and polishing.

This isn't to say that it's impossible. There are commercial sharpening fixtures for knives that will maintain a precise angle. (SEE FIGURE 5-17.) You can also make a precision knife-sharpening jig, as shown in "Sharpening Guides for Gouges and Knives" on page 67. In general, however, knives are sharpened by eyeballing the tool angle.

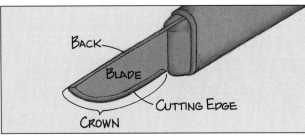

5-16 A bench knife may look simple, but this tool is the result of thousands of years of careful engineering. The *back* keeps the tool stiff, while the wedge-shaped *blade* tapers down to a thin *cutting edge* that slices through wood easily. The *crown* helps you control the cut.

5-17 This knife-sharpening fixture, available through many mail-order woodworking suppliers, guides a small stone past the knife edge. It also holds the knife so the stone always meets the cutting edge at the same angle.

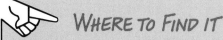

WHERE TO FIND IT

You can purchase precision knife-sharpening fixtures from:

Belcher Carving
4849 Delba Drive
Dayton, OH 45439

The most common way to grind the cutting edge of a knife is to make a *double bevel* — sharpening both surfaces of the blade at the same angle. You can also make a *single bevel* — grinding one surface flat and creating a bevel on the other. Or you can grind a *double hollow* in the edge using a grinding wheel. (SEE FIGURE 5-18.)

If you use a bench stone, hold the knife with the handle roughly perpendicular to the length of the stone. Tilt the blade at a small angle and move the knife along the stone, pressing down lightly. (SEE FIGURE 5-19.) If you use a grinding wheel, wipe the blade lightly across the circumference of the spinning abrasive, moving it roughly parallel to the axis of rotation. (SEE FIGURE 5-20.) Whether you sharpen by hand or with a machine, polish the sharpened blade on a strop with buffing compound to remove the burr.

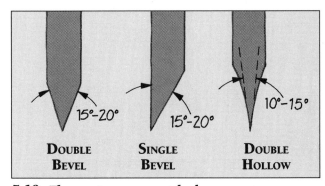

5-18 The most common method of sharpening a knife — grinding a *double bevel* on the cutting edge — also produces the most durable edge. Some craftsmen treat the knife in the same manner as a chisel. They grind one side flat, then put a *single bevel* on the other. The reasoning behind this is that it's easier to maintain one bevel angle than two. If you sharpen your knives on a grinding wheel, you probably grind a *double hollow* edge. This produces the most acute and the least durable tool angle.

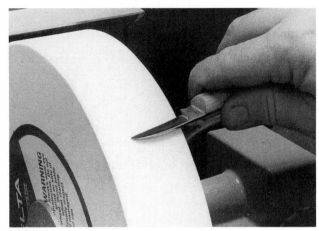

5-19 To sharpen a knife on a
stone, hold it roughly perpendicular
to the length of the stone as you move
it across the surface. Although some
craftsmen prefer to hold the stone in
one hand and the knife in the other,
this makes it doubly hard to maintain the angle. Place the stone firmly
on the bench.

5-20 To sharpen a knife on a
grinding wheel, wipe the blade
across the circumference, moving
roughly parallel to the wheel's axis.
Use very light pressure or you may
remove too much metal from the
thin blade.

SHARPENING SCRAPERS

When you scrape a surface smooth with a hand
scraper, you're cutting the wood with a burr on the
edge of the metal. (*SEE FIGURE 5-21.*) Scrapers, in fact,
have two burrs on each edge. When you wear one
out, turn the tool around and use the other.

To sharpen a scraper, you raise fine, even burrs along
the length of the edge. First remove the old burrs, if
the scraper has them, filing and grinding the edge
square. Then raise two separate burrs with a burnisher,
rolling them over at the proper angle. (*SEE FIGURES 5-22
THROUGH 5-25.*)

When a scraper is properly sharpened, it will throw
thin *curls,* similar to the shavings from a hand plane
but much thinner. You know the scraper is dull when
it won't produce anything but dust.

5-21 A scraper is a thin metal
blade with *burrs* on the edges. The
burrs are turned 75 to 80 degrees
from the face of the blade using a
burnisher. When in use, the blade is
held at an angle of 65 to 70 degrees
to the wood and the burr becomes a
cutting edge. As the scraper is pushed
forward, the burr lifts a shaving and
the blade turns it. Because the burr
is so small, it takes a very shallow
cut and leaves a smooth surface on
all sorts of wood grain.

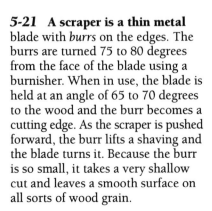

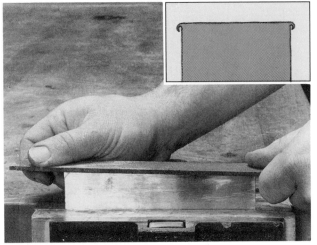

5-22 To sharpen a hand scraper, first file the cutting edges square to the face of the blade with a second-cut (medium) mill file. Some craftsmen prefer to mount the file in a saw jointer fixture to keep it perfectly square to the blade.

5-23 After filing, hone the edges with a medium sharpening stone to remove any file marks. Wipe the faces on a fine sharpening stone to remove any traces of the old burr, or any burrs left by the file.

5-24 Place the scraper flat on the workbench. Lubricate the burnisher by rubbing it with a candle or a block of paraffin wax. (This is one time when you really are lubricating a sharpening tool.) Draw the waxed burnisher along each cutting edge, pressing down hard enough that the burnisher makes a loud tick when it falls off the end of the scraper and hits the workbench. (In England, a burnisher is referred to as a *ticketer.*) Turn the scraper over and repeat. This will raise a burr on each edge.

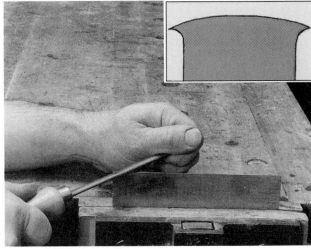

5-25 Clamp the scraper in a vise with a cutting edge up. Tilt the burnisher 10 to 15 degrees off horizontal and draw it along the edge, pressing down firmly. Then tilt the burnisher in the other direction and draw it along the edge again. Turn the scraper over and repeat for the other cutting edge. This will roll the burrs over so they are between 75 and 80 degrees from the face. **Note:** The technique for sharpening the edges of curved hand scrapers is the same, although it takes more time and patience.

SHARPENING GUIDES FOR GOUGES AND KNIVES

These special sharpening guides hold tools with complex cutting edges at precise angles to the stone. A *rotating honing guide* lets you rotate, roll, and tilt skew chisels, gouges, and V-tools at almost any angle. It also works well when sharpening ordinary flat chisels. A *knife sharpening guide* keeps a knife at a consistent angle as you wipe the blade across ordinary sandpaper.

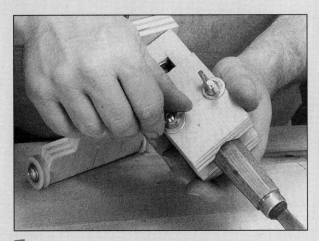

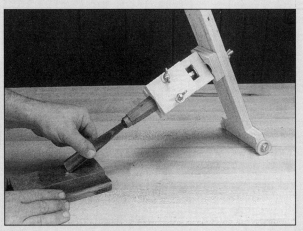

1 **To mount a tool in the** rotating honing guide, first clamp the handle in the grooved holder. Adjust the position of the holder along the support so the blade meets the stone at the proper tool angle.

2 **Grasp the tool by the blade** and apply light pressure as you rub it back and forth across the stone. If you are sharpening a skew chisel or a parting tool, rotate the tool so the bevel is flat on the stone and hold it there. If you're sharpening a gouge, roll the blade from side to side as you sharpen.

3 **To use the knife sharpening** guide, clamp the handle of the knife in the holder so the blade protrudes past the holder's edge. Depending on the condition of the knife's cutting edge, insert a coarse or medium abrasive block in the mount. Then adjust the height of the mount so the cutting edge of the knife meets the rounded surface of the abrasive at the desired angle. **Note:** Raising or lowering the mounting $1/16$ inch changes the tool angle about 1 degree.

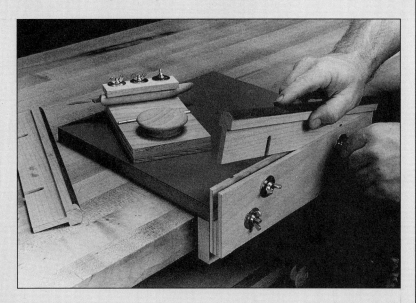

(continued) ▷

SHARPENING GUIDES FOR GOUGES AND KNIVES — CONTINUED

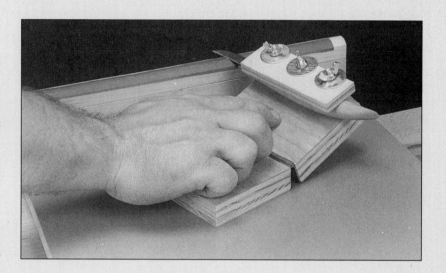

4 **Grasp the holder and move** the knife back and forth, wiping the edge of the blade across the abrasive. When you're finished with one grade of sandpaper, remove the block and replace it with another covered with a finer abrasive. Use 120-grit to grind, 320-grit to hone, and 600-grit to polish — this will finish a single bevel. If you wish to grind a double bevel, turn the knife end for end in the holder and repeat the procedure for the other side of the blade.

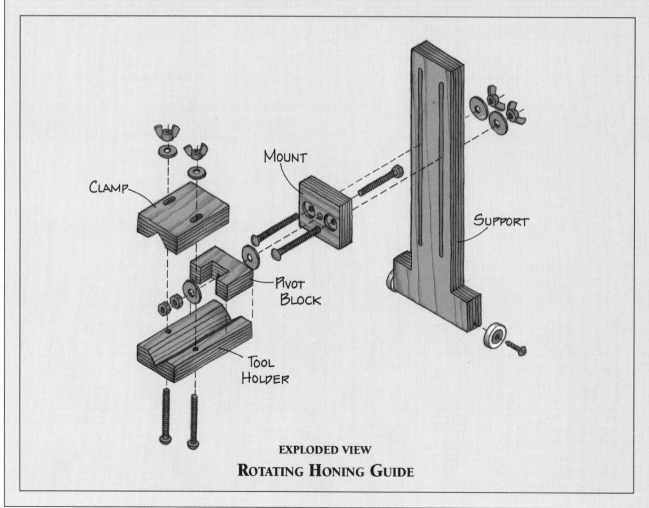

EXPLODED VIEW
ROTATING HONING GUIDE

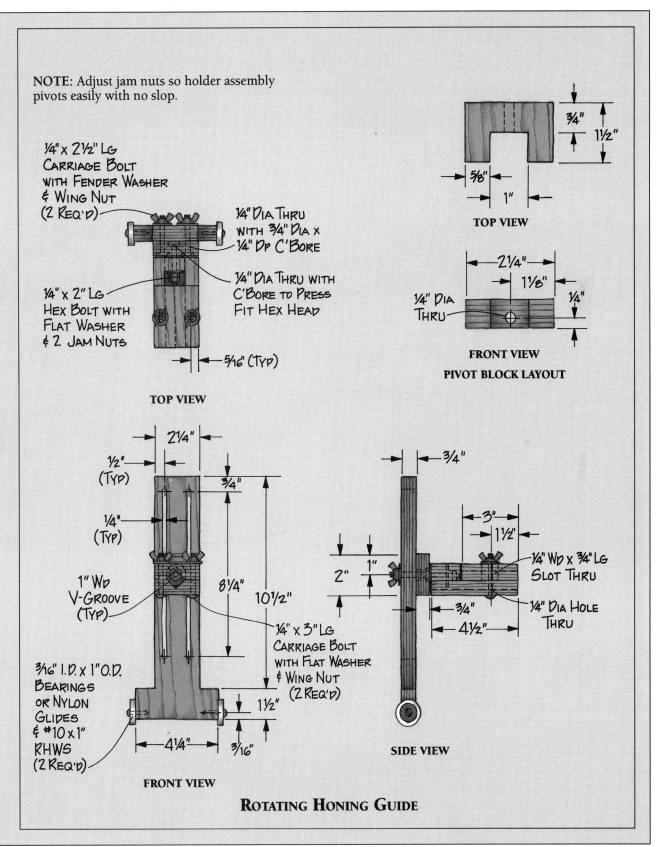

NOTE: Adjust jam nuts so holder assembly pivots easily with no slop.

¼" x 2½" LG CARRIAGE BOLT WITH FENDER WASHER & WING NUT (2 REQ'D)

¼" DIA THRU WITH ¾" DIA x ¼" DP C'BORE

¼" DIA THRU WITH C'BORE TO PRESS FIT HEX HEAD

¼" x 2" LG HEX BOLT WITH FLAT WASHER & 2 JAM NUTS

5⁄16" (TYP)

TOP VIEW

¾"

1½"

5⁄8"

1"

TOP VIEW

2¼"

1⅛"

¼" DIA THRU

¼"

FRONT VIEW

PIVOT BLOCK LAYOUT

2¼"

½" (TYP)

¾"

¼" (TYP)

1" WD V-GROOVE (TYP)

8¼"

10½"

¼" x 3" LG CARRIAGE BOLT WITH FLAT WASHER & WING NUT (2 REQ'D)

3⁄16" I.D. x 1" O.D. BEARINGS OR NYLON GLIDES & #10 x 1" RHWS (2 REQ'D)

1½"

4¼"

3⁄16"

FRONT VIEW

¾"

3"

1½"

2"

1"

¾"

4½"

¼" WD x ¾" LG SLOT THRU

¼" DIA HOLE THRU

SIDE VIEW

ROTATING HONING GUIDE

(continued) ▷

SHARPENING GUIDES FOR GOUGES AND KNIVES — CONTINUED

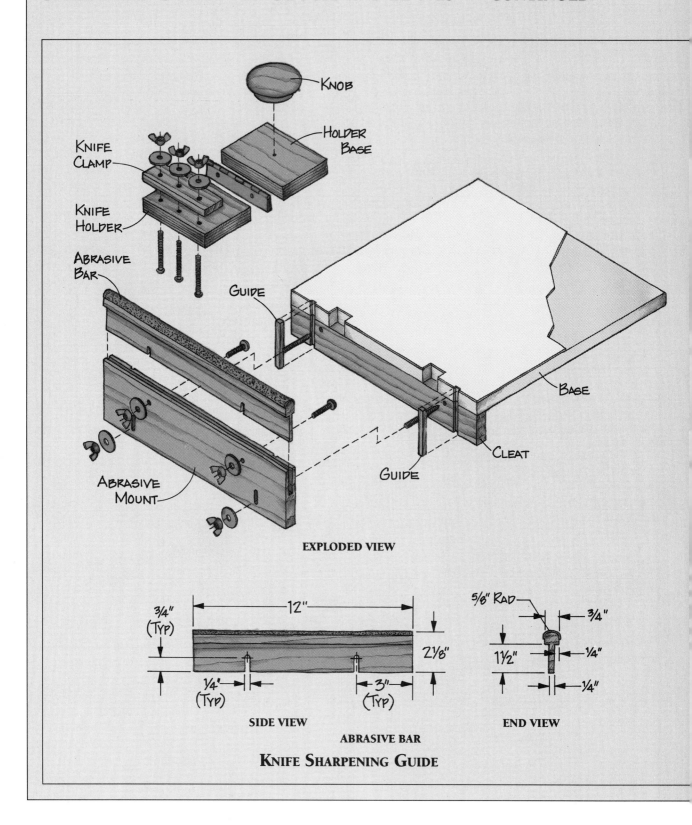

EXPLODED VIEW

SIDE VIEW

ABRASIVE BAR

END VIEW

KNIFE SHARPENING GUIDE

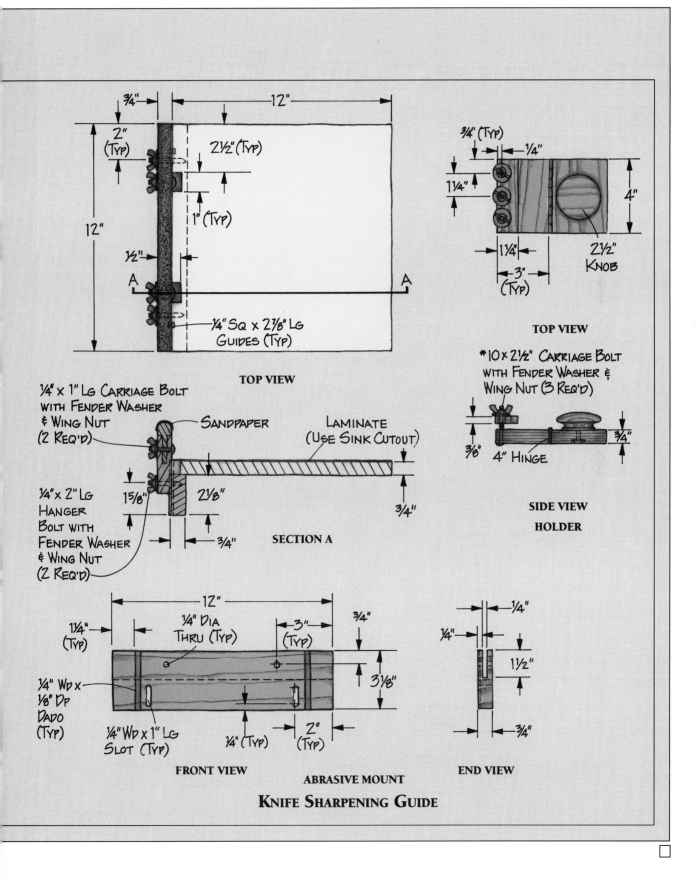

¾"

12"

2"
(Typ)

2½"(Typ)

1" (Typ)

12"

½"

A ———— A

¼" Sq x 2⅛" Lg
Guides (Typ)

TOP VIEW

¾" (Typ)

¼"

1¼"

4"

1¼"

2½"
Knob

3"
(Typ)

TOP VIEW

¼" x 1" Lg Carriage Bolt
with Fender Washer
& Wing Nut
(2 Req'd)

Sandpaper

Laminate
(Use Sink Cutout)

¼" x 2" Lg
Hanger
Bolt with
Fender Washer
& Wing Nut
(2 Req'd)

15/8"

2⅛"

¾"

¾"

SECTION A

#10 x 2½" Carriage Bolt
with Fender Washer &
Wing Nut (3 Req'd)

3/8"

4" Hinge

¾"

SIDE VIEW
HOLDER

12"

¼" Dia
Thru (Typ)

3"
(Typ)

¾"

1¼"
(Typ)

3⅛"

¼" Wd x
⅛" Dp
Dado
(Typ)

¼" Wd x 1" Lg
Slot (Typ)

¼" (Typ)

2"
(Typ)

¼"

¼"

1½"

¾"

FRONT VIEW

ABRASIVE MOUNT

END VIEW

KNIFE SHARPENING GUIDE

6

SHARPENING SAWS, BITS, AND CUTTERS

There was a time when craftsmen sharpened all of their cutting tools, but that is long past. Many cutting tools — particularly *power* tools — have become increasingly advanced and so has the technology required to sharpen them. Saws, bits, and cutters for power machinery may operate on the same principles as their hand-held cousins, but they are driven with enormous force at high speeds, which makes their tool geometry much more critical. The cutting edges are usually made with hard materials — high-speed steel or carbide — so they are more difficult to grind. Special equipment and training may be needed to sharpen them properly. For these reasons, it's more practical, economical, and safer to take machine cutters and complex cutting tools to a professional to sharpen.

However, you still have an important role in this. A professional sharpener can't put a keen edge on poorly made or worn-out tools. To get good results from a sharpener, you must invest in tools that will take and hold a sharp edge. And once you have the keen edges you crave, a little judicious cleaning and honing on your part can help preserve them.

HANDSAWS AND CIRCULAR SAWS

Sharpening a saw is more complex than simply grinding the cutting edges of the teeth. Sharpeners must perform several tasks, which differ depending on whether the tool is a handsaw or a circular saw.

SHARPENING HANDSAWS

Handsaws were sharpened without the benefit of sharpening machines for thousands of years, so you may find it strange that I recommend you take these tools to a professional. However, handsaws typically have over a hundred teeth, all of which should be ground to the same shape and angle. It's hard to justify the time it takes to file the teeth when you can pay a professional just a few dollars to do a better job.

You cannot achieve the same precision with hand files and guides that a pro can with a sharpening machine. According to one professional sharpener, "You can get some of the teeth correct, and the saw will cut better than it did when it was dull. But unless you're very good or very careful, you won't get them all. And if only some of the teeth are cutting, you'll have to work harder with that handsaw than you need to."

Still, there are times when it's handy to know how to sharpen a handsaw. (After all, your sharpener isn't open every day of the week.) You'll need a mill file, a saw jointer, a saw set, and a triangular file. *(SEE FIGURE 6-1.)* Begin by cleaning the saw — this should always be the first step in any sharpening operation — and inspecting the teeth for damage. Compare the unused teeth near the *heel* (back) of the saw with those toward

the middle. Are the used teeth worn? Are any teeth broken? This will give you a good idea of how much work you have to do.

If the teeth are extremely worn or damaged, *joint* them flat and even with a mill file — that is, file them to the same height. *(SEE FIGURE 6-2.)* When you joint, you must file down the tops of the unused teeth more than those that are already worn down. If you remove

6-2 Clean the handsaw and inspect the teeth. If the used teeth in the middle of the saw are worn down more than the teeth at the heel, or if the teeth have been damaged, joint the teeth with a mill file. Clamp the file in a saw jointer and run it along the teeth until all the teeth are at the same height. You know they're all at the same height when there's a small, shiny spot on the tops of all the teeth.

6-1 To sharpen handsaws in your own shop, you'll need a *mill file* (1) to file the teeth to the same height, a *saw jointer* (2) to hold the mill file, a *saw set* (3) to set or bend the teeth, and a *triangular file* (4) to sharpen the teeth. Triangular files are available in several widths to match the size of the saw teeth — *taper* for saws with more than 6 teeth per inch (tpi), *slim taper* for saws with 6 to 8 tpi, *extra slim taper* for saws with 10 to 16 tpi, and *double extra slim taper* for saws with extremely fine teeth. The most-common handsaws have between 8 and 12 tpi.

more than a third of the height of any one tooth, you'll have to recut or *shape* the teeth with a triangular file *(SEE FIGURES 6-3 AND 6-4.)* When you've found it necessary to shape the teeth, you must also *set* them, alternately bending them to the left and right. *(SEE FIGURE 6-5.)* Finally, *sharpen* the teeth with a fine (smooth-cut) triangular file. File ripsaws straight across and crosscut saws at an angle of 60 to 65 degrees. *(SEE FIGURE 6-6.)* **Note:** If you've never sharpened a saw before, practice on an old one before filing a good, expensive tool.

WHERE TO FIND IT

You can purchase saw sets from some mail-order tool suppliers. However, don't pay a lot of money for a tool you only need once in a great while. If you can't find a saw set for a reasonable price, look for one at flea markets, garage sales, and auctions. You can often purchase a used set for just a few dollars.

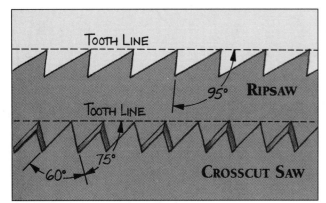

6-3 When jointing removes more than a third of the height of any of the teeth, you must also recut the teeth shapes with a triangular file. Clamp the saw between two long scraps of plywood to hold it rigid. If you're sharpening a ripsaw, hold the file so it will cut hooked teeth, with the faces about 95 degrees from the *tooth line.* (This is an imaginary line drawn across the tops of the teeth.) For a crosscut saw, hold the file to cut sloped teeth, with the faces about 75 degrees from the tooth line.

6-4 To cut all the gullets between the teeth to the same depth, align the plywood scraps about 1/16 inch below the old gullets (before filing) and parallel to the tooth line. Stop cutting when the file reaches the plywood. Inspect the teeth; they should all be pointed, with no shiny flat spots on top. If any flat spots remain, readjust the plywood scraps and file the gullets another 1/32 inch deeper. Repeat until the flat spots disappear and the teeth are all properly shaped.

6-5 Most saw teeth are slightly bent or set left or right so they will cut a kerf that's slightly wider than the body of the saw. (The rule of thumb is that the set should be about one-third the width of the saw blade.) This prevents the saw from binding in the cut. After jointing and shaping, bend the teeth with a saw set, a hand tool especially made for this purpose. Adjust the saw set, then bend every other tooth to the right. Go back and bend the teeth in between to the left.

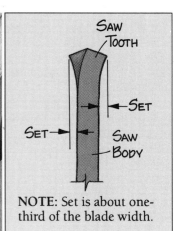

NOTE: Set is about one-third of the blade width.

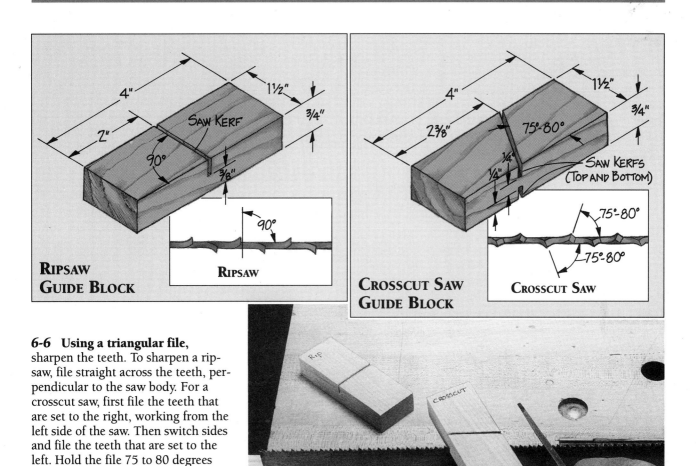

6-6 Using a triangular file, sharpen the teeth. To sharpen a ripsaw, file straight across the teeth, perpendicular to the saw body. For a crosscut saw, first file the teeth that are set to the right, working from the left side of the saw. Then switch sides and file the teeth that are set to the left. Hold the file 75 to 80 degrees from the saw body, and use a homemade guide block to help maintain the angle. **Note:** To help hold the end of the file, drill a hole in a small wood scrap and insert the end of the file in the scrap, as shown.

SHARPENING CIRCULAR SAWS

Although circular saws are designed to cut in much the same way as handsaws, they are sharpened somewhat differently. They require special sharpening equipment and skills that are beyond the capabilities of most woodworkers. Nonetheless, you may find it useful to know a little about how these tools are sharpened.

Professional sharpeners start by cleaning and polishing the blade. They then inspect it, not only for wear but also for damaged or missing teeth and cracks in the plate. If the teeth are made from high-speed steel, they will all have to be reground and reset to restore their shape and set. If the teeth are tipped with carbide, sharpeners may braze or silver solder new tips in place, matching the size and shape of the original carbide. If the blade is cracked, expect that it will be

returned to you with the bad news that you need a new one. OSHA (Occupational Health and Safety Administration) regulations prevent professionals from sharpening a blade with a cracked or broken plate.

After repairing the teeth and the plate, the sharpener checks for flatness and tension to prevent runout (wobbling) at high speeds. *(See Figure 6-7.)* Excessive runout interferes with the accuracy of the saw and increases the chances of kickback. A warped or improperly tensioned blade can be flattened or re-tensioned with a hammer and an anvil. *(See Figure 6-8.)*

You can measure the runout in your saw blades by comparing the width of the saw kerf to the width of the set or the carbide tips. If the blade has no runout, the measurements will be identical; if there is runout, the kerf will be wider than the set or the tips. A difference of .005 to .007 inch is extremely good; .010 to .015 inch is acceptable for a 10-inch blade. If the runout is more than that, inform your sharpener. The blade may need flattening or tensioning. (And then again, it may not — if the runout is consistent from blade to blade, the problem could lie with your table saw.)

Proper tensioning can also quiet a screaming blade. Blades sometimes vibrate at high frequencies as they spin, and this will cause them to scream. (Contrary to a prevalent myth, screaming is not caused by the air whistling through the gullets.) Blade stabilizers and copper plugs in the saw plate reduce the screaming by dampening the vibrations. Tensioning reduces the tendency of a spinning blade to vibrate.

Note: In order for a saw sharpener to tension a blade, the plate must be made from good-quality tool steel — softer steels won't hold the tension. If you purchase cheap blades, you may have to live with any runout or other problems that develop. Ask your sharpener to recommend blades that will hold the tension.

FOR BEST RESULTS

Shop for saw blades and other cutting tools at an industrial supplier that services contractors and other professionals in the building trades. The quality is often better than that of tools marketed to the general public, yet the prices are not that much higher.

When the blade is as flat as it can be made, the sharpener deals with the teeth. (SEE FIGURE 6-9.) Each tooth must be ground to the proper height and angle so the blade remains perfectly round.

Woodworkers sometimes ask their sharpeners to *balance* their saw blades or *polish* the sharpened surfaces with fine abrasives. Both of these requests are unnecessary and may, in fact, be detrimental to the blade.

6-7 A sharpener checks the plate with a straightedge to make sure it's flat and properly tensioned. Few blades are perfect, and even the best may be slightly warped or poorly tensioned. When mounted on a table saw arbor, these problems will cause a blade to wobble from side to side as it spins — its runout is a measure of how far it wobbles. Excessive runout can interfere with the accuracy of the cut. It can also be dangerous — a blade with too much runout is more likely to kick back.

6-8 The sharpener flattens and tensions the blade with special hammers on a highly polished anvil. To flatten a warped blade, he hits the plate so it bends in the opposite direction of the warp. To tension a blade, he taps it in such a way that it spreads out the metal in a small area. This creates tension in that immediate area. By tensioning the right spots, the sharpener counteracts the tendency of the blade to wobble and flutter when running at high speeds.

Balancing is a wasted effort on small blades (under 12 inches in diameter); they simply don't have enough mass, nor do they spin fast enough, to benefit from this technique. Additionally, to properly balance a blade, *it must be spun on its arbor.* In other words, you'd have to leave the saw blade and the saw with your sharpener! If a blade wobbles or vibrates, tensioning will cure these problems more effectively than balancing.

As for polishing, it's not necessary for a sharpener to use extra-fine abrasives to sharpen a cutting edge. The same effect can be achieved by speeding up the grinding wheel and adjusting the feed rate to a slow crawl. *(SEE FIGURE 6-10.)* Besides, fine abrasives can produce enough heat to reduce the hardness of high-speed steel teeth and crack carbide-tipped teeth.

One thing woodworkers don't ask their sharpener very often is to sharpen *new* handsaws and steel circular saw blades. However, it's often worthwhile. Straight out of the package, these tools may be serviceable, but most are not as sharp as they could be. The teeth in many new handsaws are just stamped and set. The better saws are rough-filed, but few are fully sharpened. As for new circular saw blades, they are often sandblasted *after* sharpening to give them a

bright finish. Carbide-tipped teeth remain sharp, but sandblasting dulls steel teeth slightly before they're ever used. You can use them as they are, but most new saws will cut cleaner with less work if you have them sharpened first.

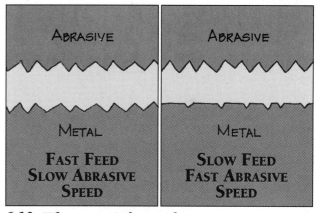

FOR YOUR INFORMATION

Manufacturers sometimes advertise that their carbide-tipped blades are honed with "microfine abrasives." This is a gimmick — note that they don't mention a grit number. Almost all carbide-tipped saws are ground with medium abrasives (220 to 320-grit); the saws would take too long to manufacture if they weren't. However, a good manufacturer can polish a surface with a medium abrasive at a fast speed and slow feed rate, just as a good sharpener can.

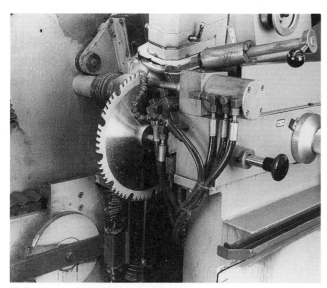

6-9 The teeth of circular saw blades are ground on the tops and the faces. Blades with steel teeth may be filed on special machines; carbide-tipped teeth should be ground under a flood of coolant to keep them from overheating. If these teeth get too hot when they are sharpened, they may crack.

ABRASIVE	ABRASIVE
METAL	METAL
FAST FEED SLOW ABRASIVE SPEED	**SLOW FEED FAST ABRASIVE SPEED**

6-10 When you grind a metal surface with a medium stone at a normal feed rate, the abrasive grains dig deep into the metal, leaving it scored and rough. However, if you speed up the stone and slow the feed rate to a crawl so just the tips of the abrasive grains cut, the score lines will be much shallower and the metal surface much smoother. This is the technique that most sharpeners use to "polish" cutting tools. It would be much too time consuming (and therefore expensive) for them to work their way through progressively finer abrasives, as you do when sharpening with a set of bench stones. What's more, the fine abrasives would generate a lot of heat, which may harm the tool.

KEEPING SAWS SHARP

You can touch up a handsaw with a triangular file of the proper size, as described on page 73. However, it's not a good idea to attack your circular saws with a file or a stone. Without special equipment, you cannot maintain the proper angles and shapes, nor can you grind the teeth evenly. There are, however, several important things you can do to keep your saws sharp.

Use the proper saw for the job. Make sure the saw is designed for the cutting you want to do. If you use an ordinary rip or crosscut blade as if it were a combination blade, then the saw has to work harder and the teeth dull faster. Use carbide-tipped saws to cut plywood and particleboard; high-speed steel cutting edges won't stand up to these tough materials.

Keep the saw clean. Oftentimes a saw that seems dull is only dirty — the wood pitch that builds up on the saw teeth keeps the cutting edges from contacting the wood. Dissolve this pitch with oven cleaner or mineral spirits. This is especially important for carbide and carbide-tipped tools, since the tannic acid in the wood residue can corrode the carbide.

6-11 To protect a handsaw or a circular saw blade when it isn't in use, cut a length of old garden hose or polyethylene tubing. Split the hose or tubing along one side and insert the teeth in the split.

Additionally, the knives must be *match ground* (ground to the same weight). If they don't all weigh the same after sharpening, the jointer or planer head won't be balanced when running at high speeds. Match grinding requires a sensitive scale.

SHARPENING KNIVES

A professional sharpener cleans the knives, checks them for damage, and measures them to see if they are all the same size and thickness. Then the blades are ground on a machine that feeds the grinding wheel across the bevel in a perfectly straight path — this leaves the cutting edge straight. (SEE FIGURE 6-12.)

Afterward, the sharpener checks the weight of the knives. If there is a large difference, the heavier knives must be ground again. After grinding, the sharpener hones and polishes the cutting edge on bench stones. (SEE FIGURE 6-13.)

Woodworkers sometimes request that the sharpener put a small *back bevel* on their jointer knives, opposite the main bevel. This decreases the cutting angle so the knives scrape the wood rather than cut it — a useful feature if you work exclusively with highly figured wood, such as curly cherry or bird's-eye maple. The scraping cut doesn't lift the grain, and there is less chipping and tearing. However, it's a useless expense for most woodworkers — back-beveled knives will not cut as smooth a surface as those that are sharpened to ordinary angles because they hammer the wood and leave pronounced mill marks. Furthermore, these knives cut slower and require more power — a 7-degree back-bevel *doubles* the horsepower needed to drive a jointer.

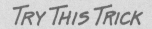

Try This Trick

Make a super cleaning paste from household lye. Dissolve 2 ounces of lye in 1 cup of distilled water, and 1 heaping tablespoon of cornstarch in 2 cups of distilled water. Add the cornstarch solution to the lye, stirring constantly. The resulting mixture will have the consistency of jelly. Apply the lye paste with an old brush, let it work for a few moments, then wipe clean with a damp rag. Wear rubber gloves and safety glasses for protection, be careful not to breathe the fumes, and store the paste in a glass container.

Protect the cutting edges. When you're not using your saws, cover the teeth to keep them from being nicked and dinged. A length of old garden hose or polyethylene tubing, split lengthwise, makes an excellent protective cover for both handsaws and circular saws. (SEE FIGURE 6-11.)

JOINTER AND PLANER KNIVES

Although jointer and planer knives have simple cutting edges, they are not especially simple to grind. You must grind the edge perfectly straight over the length of the knives — no small trick when sharpening knives from 8-inch jointers and 12-inch planers.

6-12 Jointer and planer knives are held stationary while the grinding wheel moves along the bevel. The cutting edge is ground parallel to the motion of the wheel. The sharpener *match grinds* each set of knives, removing the proper amount of metal from each knife so it will weigh the same as the others.

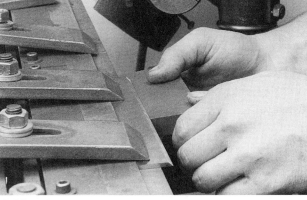

6-13 After match grinding, the cutting edges are honed and polished. Many sharpeners prefer to do this with an ordinary bench stone, as shown, rather than by machine. This saves time and doesn't overheat the knives.

KEEPING KNIVES SHARP

There are several simple dos and don'ts that will help you keep your jointer and planer knives sharp. Always clean rough lumber with a wire brush before jointing or planing because dirt acts as an abrasive and will quickly dull the knives. Remove glue beads with a glue scraper before machining glued-up stock — hard glue beads will nick the knives. Don't machine painted wood, plywood, or particleboard — the minerals in paint and the adhesives in wood products will dull the knives. Never joint or plane used lumber because an imbedded screw or nail may ruin the knives.

Keep the knives clean so built-up wood pitch doesn't prevent the knives from cutting properly. When the knives become slightly worn, you can restore the cutting edges without dismounting the knives by honing them with small slip stones. Unplug the jointer or planer, then sharpen both the bevels and the backs of the knives, feeling for the correct angle. You can also purchase special touch-up hones made especially for jointer and planer knives. (*See Figure 6-14.*)

6-14 Several commercial sharpening tools allow you to touch up jointer and planer knives without removing them from the head. The tool shown holds a coarse and a fine stone, and the plastic body serves as a guide for honing both the bevels and backs of the knives.

Try This Trick

Outfit your jointer or planer with *disposable knives.* Many sharpeners sell these knives and the holding fixtures needed to mount them in your machinery. If you do a lot of jointing and planing, disposable knives may be more economical than having your knives sharpened often. They are also much easier to mount.

ROUTER BITS AND SHAPER CUTTERS

Router bits and shaper cutters have two or more cutting *flutes*. The outside edges of the flutes scrape the wood as the bit or cutter spins, so the shape of the cut surface mirrors the shape of the flutes. These are simple cutting edges, but they require a high degree of precision to sharpen properly. The flutes must all be ground *precisely* the same; otherwise, they won't cut in unison — so it's a good idea to have them professionally sharpened.

SHARPENING BITS AND CUTTERS

A sharpener thoroughly cleans router bits and shaper cutters, then inspects and grinds them. Only *inside* faces are sharpened. A grinding wheel removes exactly the same amount of metal from each flute; this keeps them balanced. (*SEE FIGURE 6-15.*)

6-15   The sharpener only grinds the inside faces of router bits and shaper cutters. This preserves the diameter and shape of the tool.

6-16   To touch up the cutting edges of router bits and shaper cutters, rub only the *inside* faces across a fine bench stone. Don't use a coarse stone; you may remove too much metal. Use a diamond stone if the tool is made from or tipped with carbide; use either ceramic or diamond stones for cutters made of high-speed steel. Count the strokes as you sharpen, and stroke each flute across the stone the same number of times. This way, you'll remove approximately the same amount of metal from each flute and the flutes will remain balanced.

Except to clean the cutting tools, the sharpener rarely touches the outside faces. This would alter the diameter and possibly the shape. Depending on the design, grinding away metal from the inside faces may reduce the diameter, but only microscopically; under normal circumstances, this slight reduction isn't enough to matter.

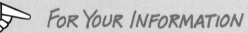

FOR YOUR INFORMATION

Some sharpeners offer to plate router and drill bits with gold-colored titanium nitride as a special service. You can also purchase plated bits. There is some controversy surrounding titanium plating — some craftsmen report that plated edges stay sharp longer; others say it isn't worth the expense. How well a plated edge performs depends on how it's used. Titanium nitride reduces the friction at the cutting edge, helping the bit run cooler. This is especially helpful when cutting metals. It's less effective when working wood, and probably isn't worthwhile unless you use the bits often and for long periods of time. Plating is worthless if you cut abrasive materials such as plywood, particleboard, and fiberboard — these quickly wear away the titanium.

KEEPING BITS AND CUTTERS SHARP

To keep router bits and shaper cutters sharp, avoid *hogging* the cut — don't try to remove too much stock at once. Take light cuts, removing no more than 1/8 to 1/4 inch of stock in a single pass. Although it takes longer to complete a cut with this technique, the bits

and cutters don't have to work as hard and they stay sharp longer. They also run cooler, which reduces the chance that you might overheat a bit and alter its hardness.

Be sure to keep bits and cutters clean. Because they operate at much higher speeds than other cutting tools, wood pitch builds up on their cutting edges more quickly. As pitch builds up on the outside of the bit or cutter, it causes more friction, and the resulting heat increases the chance of overheating the tool.

You can touch up the cutting edges of bits and cutters by rubbing the inside faces of the flutes across a bench stone or a slip stone. (SEE FIGURE 6-16.) Use a fine stone so you won't score the surfaces or remove much metal. Sharpen each flute the same amount to keep the tool balanced. Remember — *never sharpen the outside surfaces of a router bit or shaper cutter.*

Note: You can use this same technique to touch up the cutting edges of other fluted cutters, such as countersinks and molding knives.

Drill Bits

There are four types of machine drill bits commonly used in woodworking — spade bits, twist bits, bradpoint bits, and Forstner bits. Because each of these cuts the wood in a different manner, each must be sharpened differently.

SHARPENING SPADE BITS AND TWIST BITS

Although a sharpener may be able to do the job in less time, two of these bits can be effectively sharpened in a home workshop — spade bits and twist bits. Spade bits have two flutes that scrape the wood. The edges of the flutes are ground at a slight angle. With a simple jig to help maintain this angle, you can file each flute and restore the cutting edge. (SEE FIGURES 6-17 AND 6-18.) However, you must be careful to file them evenly.

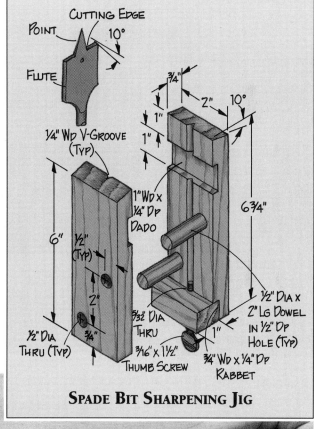

SPADE BIT SHARPENING JIG

6-17 To sharpen a spade bit, first file the bottom edges of the flutes. You must hold the file at a 10-degree angle. Additionally, both flutes must be filed precisely the same, so the ears (outside corners) are even with one another. To help guide the file and keep the flutes even, make the jig shown. Clamp the bit in the jig and adjust the stop so the edge of the flutes are about 1/64 inch above the top surface of the jig. Lay a mill file on the top surface and file the flute until the edge is even with the jig. Repeat for the second flute.

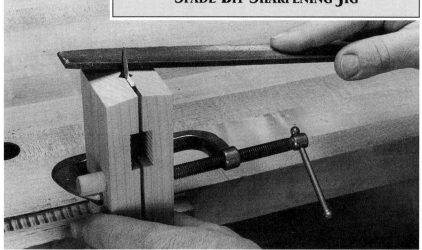

There are several inexpensive commercial sharpening fixtures for twist bits. (SEE FIGURE 6-19.) Still, many woodworkers find it's not cost effective to sharpen small-diameter bits, below 3/16 inch in diameter — they are cheap enough that they can be replaced for less trouble than it takes to sharpen them. However, if you use larger twist drills often, it may be worth your while to invest in a sharpening fixture.

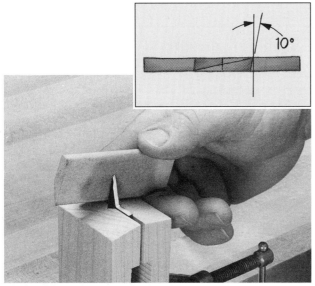

6-18 After filing the flutes, *lightly* hone the sides of the points with a medium slip stone. Hold the stone angled back about 10 degrees, as shown. Count your strokes and hone each side the same amount to keep the point centered. *Don't hone too much!* Each side should only take five or six strokes of the stone.

6-19 Twist bits have complex cutting edges, as you can see. Nevertheless, there are several inexpensive commercial fixtures that will put a serviceable edge on these bits. Some have their own built-in motors; others fasten to a portable electric drill; the one shown works with a grindstone or a sander. When sharpening, you may want to change the angle of the *lips* depending on the material you're drilling. Grind at 45 to 55 degrees for wood, 59 to 70 degrees for metal, and 30 to 40 degrees for plastic. Be careful to grind both lips the same amount so the point remains centered.

TOUCHING UP BRAD-POINT BITS AND FORSTNER BITS

The cutting edges of brad-point and Forstner bits are much more complex than those of spade and twist bits. Consequently, they require more time and precision to sharpen. It's best to let a pro completely sharpen them when they become worn. However, you can easily touch up the cutting edges between sharpenings.

Use an auger bit file to touch up the spurs and lips of a brad-point drill bit, provided they're made from carbon tool steel; use a ceramic file if they're made from high-speed steel. (SEE FIGURES 6-20 AND 6-21.) To restore a slightly worn Forstner bit, lightly hone the leading and trailing faces of the lifters and both halves of the rim. (SEE FIGURES 6-22 AND 6-23.) *Don't* sharpen the outside surfaces of the bit; you'll change the diameter.

TRY THIS TRICK

Ask your sharpener to grind brad points in a set of high-speed steel twist drills. This may be somewhat expensive, but it will make a better, longer-lasting, and more versatile set than you can buy. Commercial brad-point bit sets don't have as many sizes as twist-bit sets, and they are usually made from carbon tool steel, which isn't as wear-resistant or as heat-resistant as high-speed steel.

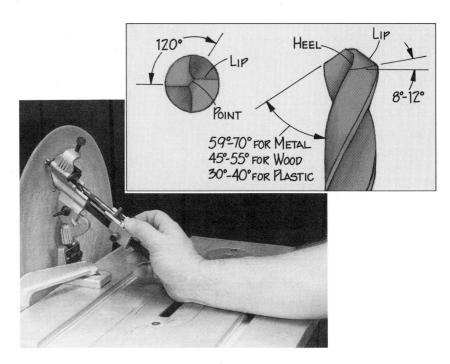

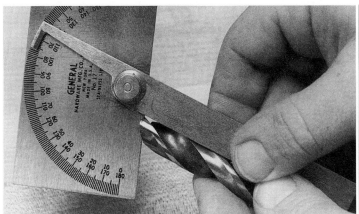

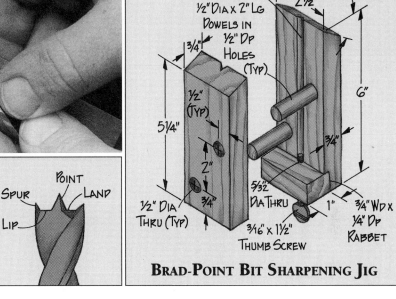

BRAD-POINT BIT SHARPENING JIG

6-20 Before touching up the edge of a brad-point bit, measure the angle of the bottom edges (called the *lands*) with a protractor. The angle of each land should be about 70 degrees. Make a simple jig to hold the bit and help guide the files, as shown. Bevel the ends of the jig to match the angle of the land.

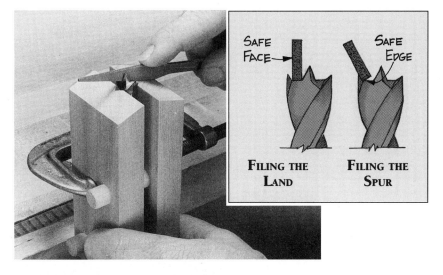

6-21 Clamp the bit in the jig, aligning the lands with the angled end. Take a good look at your auger bit file — note that one end has safe edges while the other end has safe faces. (A *safe* file surface has no teeth.) Touch up the lands using the file end with safe faces; rest the file on the angled ends of the jig to help guide it. Then touch up the *inside* edges of the spurs using the file end with safe edges. **Note:** *Don't file the outside surfaces of the spurs.*

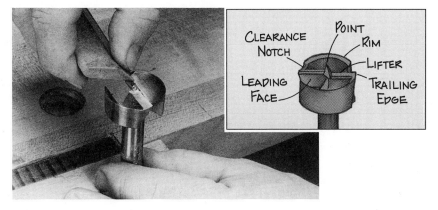

6-22 To touch up a Forstner bit, use a small, fine slip stone to hone both the leading and trailing faces of each *lifter.* Hone the leading face first, pressing the stone flat against the surfaces. Then hone the trailing faces — the clearance notches on each side of the bit will let you reach these surfaces with a small stone. Count your strokes and hone each side of the bit evenly.

KEEPING DRILL BITS SHARP

Like other machine cutters, drill bits must be kept clean and free of wood pitch to cut well. However, the most important thing you can do to keep your bits sharp is to *run them at the proper speed.* Many novices run drill bits too fast. As a result, the bits can't clear the chips from the hole fast enough and they begin to bind up. This, in turn, overheats the bit; it also loses some of its hardness and doesn't hold its edge as long.

As a rule of thumb, run brad-point bits and twist bits at 1,200 rpm or less. If you're using a twist bit to drill metal or plastic, it should turn slower than that, at about 500 rpm. Run spade bits and Forstner bits between 400 and 800 rpm. The larger the bit, the slower it should rotate.

6-23 Using the rounded end of the slip stone, hone the *inside* edge of the *rim.* Roll the bit back and forth in your fingers while holding the rim against the stone. *Don't* hone the outside of the rim; you'll change the diameter of the bit.

FINDING A GOOD SHARPENER

Just as it makes good sense to buy good-quality cutting tools, you should take them to a good sharpener. But how can you tell the good professionals from the mediocre? There are several things to look for.

Equipment — Look for a well-equipped shop. Does the sharpener have grinding machines designed to handle the cutters you want sharpened? Are they automated? (Some of the best grinding machines are computer controlled, although there are plenty of good sharpeners who haven't yet joined the computer revolution.) Can the sharpener wet grind, under a flood of coolant? This is especially important if you have carbide or carbide-tipped tools to be sharpened — too much heat from grinding will crack carbide.

Also look for a *proper* smithing anvil, not just an old blacksmith's horn or a piece of railroad track, that's ground and polished. The hammers, too, should be polished smithing hammers. This is an indication that the sharpener is knowledgeable and has invested in the equipment to do the job right.

Don't be put off by bench stones and other hand sharpening tools scattered among the smithing anvils and computer-controlled grinders. This is actually a good sign. Just as an experienced woodworker finds it easier to perform some tasks with hand tools rather than with power tools, an experienced sharpener may prefer to use simple tools for some sharpening chores.

Experience — Ask how long the sharpener has been in business and if this is a full-time or part-time job. You might also inquire about training or how the craft was learned. Beware of the sharpener whose only source of information is the owner's manuals that came with the sharpening machines.

Communication — Good sharpeners won't sit still for all these questions without asking a few of their own. They will probably ask you questions about the sort of woodworking you do, the sort of machinery you own, and the kind of materials you like to use. This isn't just chit-chat. It's vital information that they need to do their job properly. Experienced sharpeners can match the grind angles on saw blades and other cutters to the job, machine, and materials.

PROJECTS

7

FLAT GRINDER

You can build a sharpening machine that's as good as or better than one you can buy, as this flat grinder illustrates. It does the same job as a motorized whetstone — grinds a flat surface on a cutting tool — and offers several unique features as well.

This grinder has a simple mounting system for interchangeable tool rests, so you change the rest to fit the tool. Make the universal tool rest shown on page 104, or design special rests for specific tools. The abrasive discs are also interchangeable, allowing you to quickly change from one grade to another. Although you may have to remove the tool rest to change discs, you can do so *without changing the tool angle*. This lets you maintain the same precise setup as you work your way through finer and finer abrasives.

The abrasive discs are just ordinary sheets of sandpaper mounted to fiberboard, making them inexpensive and easy to maintain. Furthermore, you can use these abrasives *without liquids* of any type. On the opposite side of the abrasive disc from the tool rest mount is a clamping system. This holds several bench stones so you can switch between machine sharpening and hand sharpening as needed.

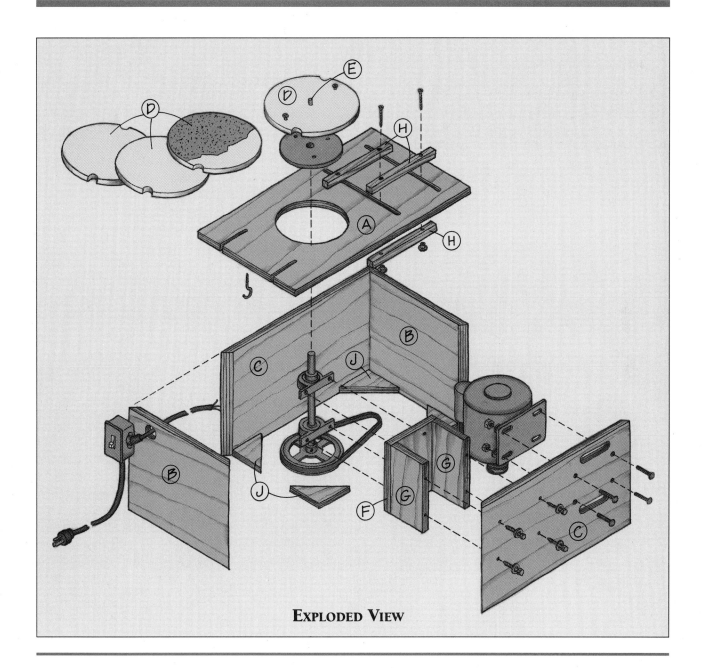

EXPLODED VIEW

MATERIALS LIST (FINISHED DIMENSIONS)

Parts

A. Top $3/4''$ x $13^1/2''$ x $23^3/4''$
B. Sides (2) $3/4''$ x $12''$ x $13^1/2''$
C. Front/back (2) $3/4''$ x $12''$ x $20''$
D. Discs* (4 or 5) $9''$ dia. x $1/2''$
E. Centering pin† $3/16''$ dia. x $1''$
F. Shaft mount
   base $3/4''$ x $6^1/4''$ x $8^1/4''$
G. Shaft mount
   risers (2) $3/4''$ x $4^1/8''$ x $8^1/4''$

H. Clamp
   bars† (4) $5/8''$ x $3/4''$ x $8^1/2''$
J. Corner braces (4) $3/4''$ x $4''$ x $4''$

*Make these parts from medium-density
fiberboard (MDF).
†Make these parts from hardwood.

Hardware

Structural

$3/8''$ x $1^1/2''$ Carriage bolts (4)
$5/16''$ x $1^1/4''$ Carriage bolts (4)
$1/4''$ x $2''$ Lag screws (4)
$1/4''$ x $2''$ Flathead machine
  screws (4)
#12 x $3/4''$ Panhead screws (3–6)
#12 x $5/8''$ Panhead screws (2)

(continued) ▷

MATERIALS LIST — CONTINUED
Hardware — CONTINUED

Structural

#8 x ¹/₂″ Panhead screws (2)
#8 x 2″ Flathead wood screws (22)
³/₈″ Hex nuts (4)
⁵/₁₆″ Hex nuts (4)
¹/₄″ T-nuts (4)
⁵/₁₆″ Flat washers (8)
¹/₄″ Flat washers (4)
¹/₈″ x 2″ Screw hook

Drive train

⁵/₈″ I.D. Locking pillow blocks (2)
2″ dia. Pulley
6″ dia. Pulley
6″ O.D. x ⁵/₈″ I.D. Faceplate
⁵/₈″ dia. x 11¹/₈″ Steel shaft
34″ V-belt

Electrical

¹/₄-hp, 1,725-rpm, 115-v Motor
     with 56 NEMA frame, clockwise
     rotation at shaft end
Electrical box with cover
Straight cord clamp
Right-angle cord clamp
14-3 Electrical cord (8′)
Grounding plug
On/off switch
Wire terminals (as required)
Cord clip

PLAN OF PROCEDURE

1 Gather the materials and cut the wooden parts to size. The flat grinder is essentially a box with a motor and a drive shaft mounted inside. Most of the parts are made from ³/₄-inch cabinet-grade plywood — you'll need about half a sheet. You'll also need less than a quarter sheet of ¹/₂-inch MDF to make the discs and a scrap of ³/₄-inch-thick hardwood for the clamp bars. Purchase the common hardware at a hardware store, where you can also order an electric motor and pillow blocks. Or pick up an electric motor at an electrical supply house and buy pillow blocks from a supplier of bearings and bushings.

WHERE TO FIND IT

Purchase the lathe faceplate from:
Total Shop
P.O. Box 25429
Greenville, SC 29616

When you have gathered all the materials, cut the wooden parts to the sizes given in the Materials List. Miter the adjoining ends of the front, back, and sides at 45 degrees. Also miter one side of each corner brace at 45 degrees to form a right triangle.

2 Cut the holes and slots. Lay out the locations of the holes and slots on the top, back, clamp bars, and shaft mount base, as shown in the *Top Layout,*

Back Layout, Clamp Bar Detail, and Shaft Mount Base Layout. Cut or drill these holes:

■ A 7-inch-diameter hole in the top to accommodate the lathe faceplate
■ ³/₈-inch-diameter holes in the shaft mount base to mount the pillow blocks
■ ⁵/₁₆-inch-diameter holes in the back to mount the motor
■ ⁵/₁₆-inch-diameter holes in the two lower clamp bars to install the T-nuts
■ ¹/₄-inch-diameter countersunk holes in the two upper clamp bars for the machine screws
■ ¹/₄-inch-diameter holes in the back to attach the shaft mount assembly
Then cut or rout these slots:
■ 1-inch-wide, 5-inch-long slots in the back to provide ventilation for the motor
■ ³/₈-inch-wide, 10¹/₈-inch-long slots in the top to mount the clamp bars
■ ³/₈-inch-wide, 3³/₁₆-inch-long slots in the top to mount tool rests

3 Cut the discs. You'll need three or four abrasive discs (for different grades of abrasives) and one mounting disc to hold them. To make these, draw the disc circumference on the stock with a compass. Mark the locations of the finger grooves around the circumferences of the discs, as shown in the *Abrasive Disc Layout* and *Mounting Disc Layout.* Drill a ³/₁₆-inch-diameter hole through the center of the disc stock, and drill 1-inch-diameter holes at the finger groove

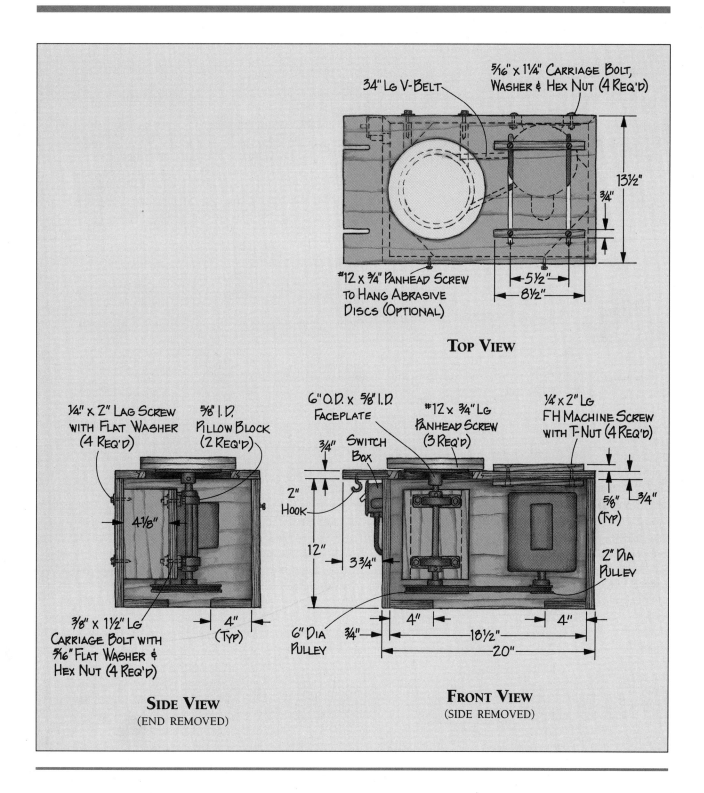

34" Lg V-Belt

⁵⁄₁₆" x 1¼" Carriage Bolt,
Washer & Hex Nut (4 Req'd)

13½"

¾"

#12 x ¾" Panhead Screw
to Hang Abrasive
Discs (Optional)

5½"
8½"

Top View

¼" x 2" Lag Screw
with Flat Washer
(4 Req'd)

⁵⁄₈" I.D.
Pillow Block
(2 Req'd)

6" O.D. x ⁵⁄₈" I.D.
Faceplate

#12 x ¾" Lg
Panhead Screw
(3 Req'd)

¼" x 2" Lg
FH Machine Screw
with T-Nut (4 Req'd)

¾"

Switch
Box

2"
Hook

12"

⁵⁄₈"
(Typ)

¾"

4⅛"

3¾"

2" Dia
Pulley

⅜" x 1½" Lg
Carriage Bolt with
⁵⁄₁₆" Flat Washer &
Hex Nut (4 Req'd)

4"
(Typ)

6" Dia
Pulley

¾"

4"

18½"

4"

20"

Side View
(End Removed)

Front View
(Side Removed)

locations. After you cut the discs, the 1-inch-diameter holes will form half-round grooves.

Using a ³⁄₁₆-inch-diameter dowel or bolt to align the center holes, stack the disc stock face to face, adhering the boards with double-faced carpet tape. Cut the circumference of the discs with a band saw or a saber saw, sawing the entire stack at once. Make the *Disc Sanding and Routing Jig,* and use it to sand the stacked discs perfectly round. (*See Figure 7-1.*) Take the stack apart and discard the tape.

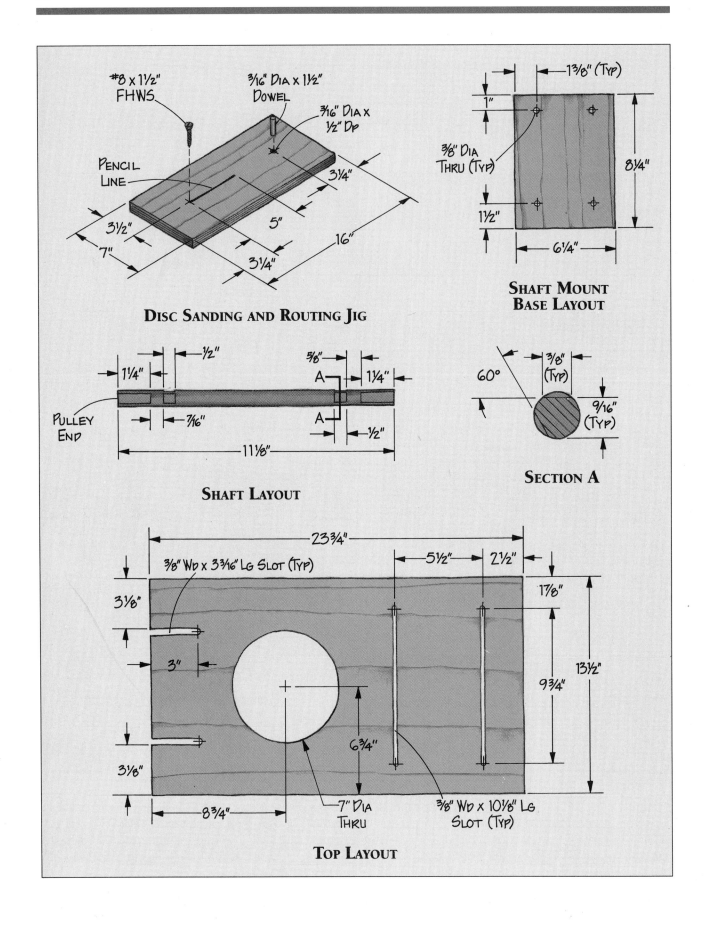

#8 x 1½"
FHWS

3/16" DIA x 1½"
DOWEL

3/16" DIA x
½" DP

PENCIL
LINE

3½"

7"

3¼"

5"

3¼"

16"

DISC SANDING AND ROUTING JIG

1 3/8" (TYP)

1"

3/8" DIA
THRU (TYP)

8¼"

1½"

6¼"

**SHAFT MOUNT
BASE LAYOUT**

1¼"

½"

5/8"

A

1¼"

PULLEY
END

7/16"

A

½"

11 1/8"

SHAFT LAYOUT

60°

3/8"
(TYP)

9/16"
(TYP)

SECTION A

23¾"

3/8" WD x 3 3/16" LG SLOT (TYP)

5½"

2½"

3 1/8"

1 7/8"

3"

13½"

9¾"

6¾"

3 1/8"

8¾"

7" DIA
THRU

3/8" WD x 10 1/8" LG
SLOT (TYP)

TOP LAYOUT

4   Cut the slots and install the screws in the discs. The abrasive discs fasten to the mounting disc with panhead screws and T-slots. Lay out the location of the slots on the abrasive discs, as shown in the *Abrasive Disc Layout,* and the screws on the mounting disc, as shown in the *Mounting Disc Layout.* Also mark where the slots begin and end on the circumference of the abrasive discs.

Drill ¹/₂-inch-diameter, ³/₈-inch-deep starting holes at the beginning of each slot. Mount a ¹/₂-inch T-slot cutter in a table-mounted router. Using the *Disc Sand-* *ing and Routing Jig* to guide the discs (as shown in FIGURE 7-2), rout the curved T-slots as shown in *Section B.*

WHERE TO FIND IT

Purchase the ¹/₂-inch T-slot cutter from:

Cascade Tools
P.O. Box 3110
Bellingham, WA 98227

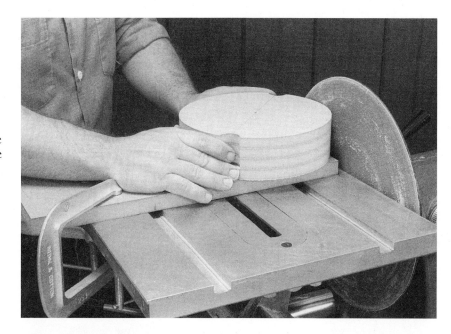

7-1   After sawing the stacked discs, you must sand the edges to make them perfectly round. Place the stack over the pivot dowel on the *Disc Sanding and Routing Jig.* Rest the jig on the table of a disc sander or belt sander, turn on the sander, and feed the discs into the sander to make a *tiny* flat spot. Turn off the sander and clamp the jig to the table. Turn on the sander again and rotate the stack on the pivot dowel, sanding away a little stock from the edges. Loosen the clamp, sand another flat spot, and repeat until you have removed all the saw marks.

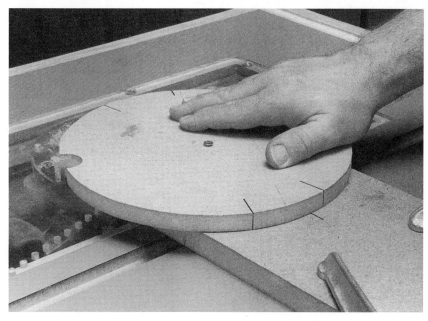

7-2   To rout the curved T-slots in an abrasive disc, use a table-mounted router and a T-slot cutter. Mount the disc to the *Disc Sanding and Routing Jig* with a #8 flathead wood screw. Line up the marks — one on the edge of the disc, to indicate the beginning of a slot, and the other on the jig. Rest the jig on the router table with the stopped hole at the beginning of the slot over the cutter. Adjust the depth of cut so the cutter just touches the bottom of the hole. Clamp the jig to the router table, turn on the router, and rotate the disc until the mark that indicates the end of the slot lines up with the mark on the jig. Turn off the router, wait for it to come to a complete stop, and disengage the disc from the cutter. Repeat this procedure for each slot.

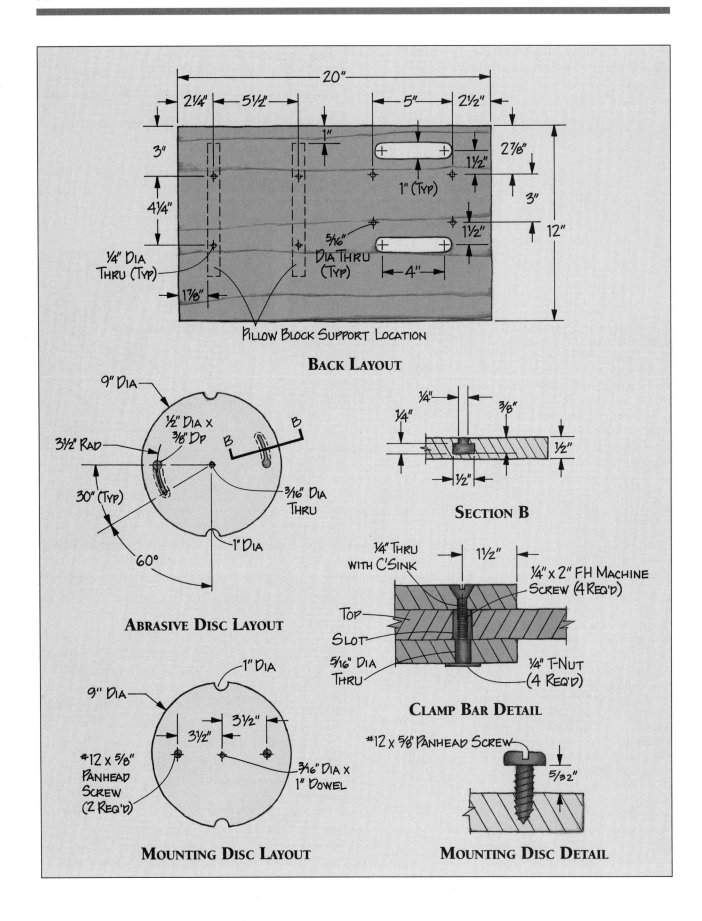

BACK LAYOUT

ABRASIVE DISC LAYOUT

SECTION B

CLAMP BAR DETAIL

MOUNTING DISC LAYOUT

MOUNTING DISC DETAIL

Drill ⅛-inch-diameter pilot holes for the panhead screws in the mounting disc, then install the screws, as shown in the *Mounting Disc Detail*. Also glue the centering pin in the center hole.

Check that the abrasive discs fasten to and detach from the mounting disc easily. Hold an abrasive disc over the mounting disc so the center hole and the slots line up with the centering pin and the screws. Drop the abrasive disc onto the mounting disc and turn it counterclockwise. Remove the abrasive disc, turning it clockwise and lifting it up. If *all* the discs seem hard to mount, check the position of the panhead screws on the mounting disc. If just one or two of the abrasive discs are stubborn, enlarge the slots *slightly* with a file.

5 Assemble and finish the box. Finish sand the wooden parts. Glue the front, back, and sides together. Before the glue dries, glue the corner braces in place and secure them with flathead wood screws. Glue the top to the assembly, and secure it with screws. Countersink all screws.

Glue and screw the shaft mount base to the shaft mount risers. Temporarily fasten the shaft mount assembly to the back of the grinder assembly with ¼-inch lag screws and washers, but *don't* glue the two assemblies together.

Remove the shaft mount assembly from the back. Do any necessary touch-up sanding, and apply tung oil or Danish oil to all wooden surfaces, including the clamp bars, abrasive discs, and mounting disc.

6 Install the drive train. File flats on the steel shaft, as shown in the *Shaft Layout*. Mount the shaft in the pillow blocks, but don't lock it in place yet. Fasten the pillow blocks to the shaft mount assembly with ⅜-inch carriage bolts, and install the 6-inch pulley on the lower end.

Secure the shaft mount assembly to the back. Attach the mounting disc to the lathe faceplate with #12 panhead screws, taking care to center the disc on the faceplate. Then install the faceplate on the upper end of the shaft. Adjust the vertical position of the shaft, so the mounting disc is about ⅛ inch above the top, and tighten the locking screws in the pillow blocks.

7 Install the motor. Decide where you want to install the switch on the grinder. As shown, it's on the right side, just under the top overhang. However, you may prefer to mount it somewhere else. Mark the position of the electrical switch box on the grinder, and

drill a 1-inch-diameter hole next to it for the wiring. Install a right-angle cord clamp in the side of the electrical box and a straight cord clamp in the lower end. Attach the electrical box to the grinder with #8 panhead screws, so the right-angle cord clamp protrudes through the 1-inch-diameter hole.

Using ring connectors, attach one end of the electrical cord to the motor. Run the cord to the electrical box and pull all but 2 feet of the cord through the right-angle clamp. Carefully pare away the plastic covering from a 3-inch-long section of cord just inside the box. Snip the line (black) wire *only* in two, strip away the insulation from the ends, and attach the cut ends to a switch.

Run the free end of the cord out of the electrical box through the straight cord clamp. Attach the switch to the box cover, then attach the box cover to the electrical box. Install a grounded plug on the free end of the cord.

Attach the motor to the back with 5/16-inch carriage bolts, but don't tighten the nuts on the ends of the bolts yet. Install a 2-inch pulley on the motor arbor and loop the V-belt over the pulleys. Slide the motor sideways until the belt is tensioned, then tighten the nuts.

8 Install the clamp bars. Install T-nuts in the 5/16-inch-diameter holes in the lower clamp bars. Turn the grinder so it rests on its front. Hold a lower clamp bar against the bottom face of the top, under the clamp bar slots. Drive ¼-inch flathead machine screws through the holes in an upper clamp bar, through the slots in the top, and into the T-nuts in the lower bar, as shown in the *Clamp Bar Detail*. Repeat for the other set of clamp bars.

9 Install the hanger screws and hook. If you wish, install two or three panhead screws in the front or the sides of the grinder, as you did in the mounting disc, to hang the extra abrasive discs when not in use. You may also wish to install a screw hook near the electrical box, to store coiled electrical cord when you're not using the grinder.

10 Mount abrasive sheets on the discs. Cut 9-inch-diameter discs from aluminum oxide or silicon-carbide sandpaper and mount them to the abrasive discs with spray adhesive. Use 120-grit for grinding, 320-grit for honing, and 600-grit for polishing. If you wish, you can also make a buffing disc by gluing a piece of leather or typing paper to an abrasive disc, then loading it with buffing compound.

USING THE FLAT GRINDER

Use the flat grinder just as you would a motorized whetstone. Hold the tool gently against the rotating disc to grind a flat surface, working your way through progressively finer abrasives to finish the cutting edge. If the cutting edge is badly damaged or misshapen, start with the coarse (120-grit) abra-sive. If it's slightly dulled, start with the medium (320-grit) abrasive. To touch up the edge, use the fine (600-grit) abrasive or the buffing wheel. When the abrasives become worn, peel up the old sand-paper and stick down a new disc.

1 **Use a tool rest to maintain** a precise tool angle as you sharpen. The universal tool rest shown mounts in the slots in the top and will handle most flat chisels and plane irons. Add guide blocks for skew chisels, gouges, and V-tools. (Plans for this tool rest are on page 104.) You can also devise your own special tool rests and mount them in the same slots.

2 **When you change abrasives,** you may have to remove the tool rest. Loosen the mounting nuts and slide the rest off the grinder. How-ever, *don't change the tool angle —* leave it as it is. Switch the abrasive discs, then replace the tool rest. The angle will stay precisely the same as you work your way through the abrasives.

8

HOLLOW GRINDER

This shopmade grinder is designed to overcome the three limitations common to most commercial hollow-grinding machines. First, commercial machines typically turn at 3,450 rpm, much too fast for grinding tool steel. At this high speed, heat from abrasive friction can build up in seconds and reduce the hardness of the steel. In contrast, this hollow grinder turns at less than 600 rpm. It takes longer to grind the tool, but the steel is less likely to overheat.

Second, most grinding wheels are narrower than plane irons, so to grind a straight edge, you must devise a fixture to draw the tool across the stone. This machine, however, turns a 5-inch-wide abrasive drum. You can mount two grades of abrasives, each 2½ inches wide, and still have room to grind a plane iron on *each* abrasive.

Finally, few commercial machines will mount abrasive wheels for both grinding and buffing. On this model, you can attach a strip of abrasive and a strip of leather to the drum, if you wish, to allow grinding on one side and buffing on the other. Or you can mount commercial grindstones and buffing wheels to the end of the drum shaft.

There is one more advantage. The front of the housing is slotted so you can mount a variety of tool rests, including the universal tool rest, shown on page 104. Or you can create your own tool rests and holding fixtures.

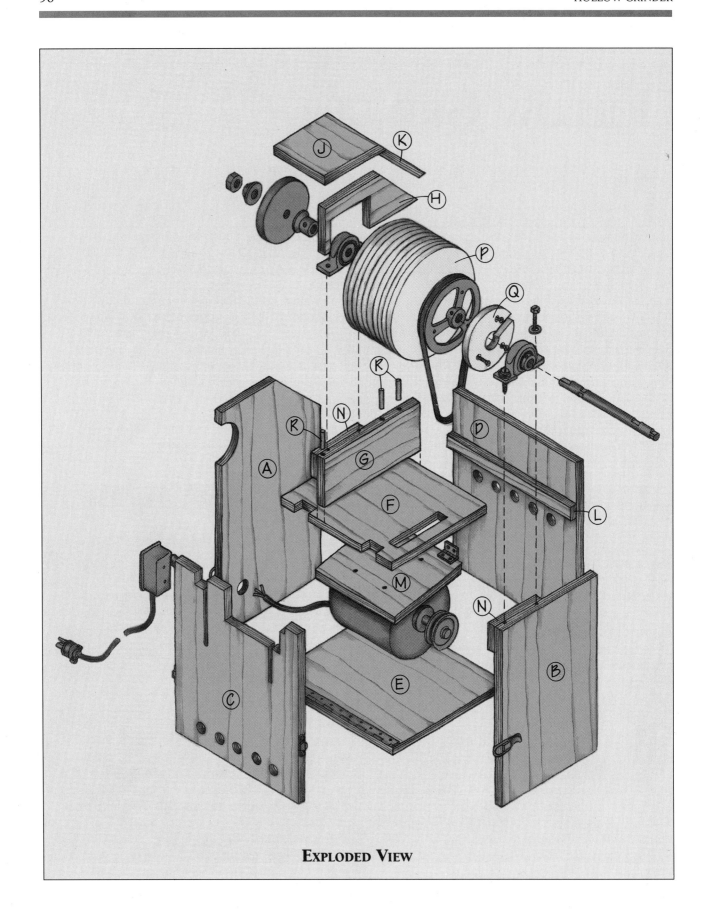

EXPLODED VIEW

MATERIALS LIST (FINISHED DIMENSIONS)

Parts

A. Left side $\frac{3}{4}''$ x $10\frac{1}{2}''$ x $20\frac{1}{2}''$
B. Right side $\frac{3}{4}''$ x $10\frac{1}{2}''$ x $16''$
C. Front $\frac{3}{4}''$ x $13\frac{1}{2}''$ x $15\frac{7}{8}''$
D. Back $\frac{3}{4}''$ x $13\frac{1}{2}''$ x $16''$
E. Bottom $\frac{3}{4}''$ x $12''$ x $13\frac{1}{2}''$
F. Shelf $\frac{3}{4}''$ x $10\frac{1}{2}''$ x $12''$
G. Partition
   bottom $\frac{3}{4}''$ x $4\frac{1}{4}''$ x $10\frac{1}{2}''$
H. Partition
   top $\frac{3}{4}''$ x $4\frac{1}{2}''$ x $10\frac{1}{2}''$
J. Guard top $\frac{3}{4}''$ x $5\frac{1}{4}''$ x $7\frac{1}{16}''$
K. Guard back $\frac{3}{4}''$ x $5\frac{1}{4}''$ x $6\frac{15}{16}''$
L. Ledger $\frac{3}{4}''$ x $1''$ x $12''$
M. Motor mount $\frac{3}{4}''$ x $8''$ x $8\frac{1}{2}''$
N. Pillow block
   mounts (2) $\frac{3}{4}''$ x $2''$ x $5\frac{1}{2}''$
P. Drum discs* (10) $9''$ dia. x $\frac{1}{2}''$
Q. Pulley mounting
   plate* $5''$ dia. x $\frac{1}{2}''$
R. Dowels (3) $\frac{3}{16}''$ dia. x $1''$

*Make these parts from medium-density
fiberboard (MDF).

Hardware

Structural

$\frac{3}{8}''$ x $2''$ Lag screws (4)
$\frac{5}{16}''$ x $1''$ Carriage bolts (4)
$\frac{1}{4}''$ x $2''$ Carriage bolts (2)
#12 x $2''$ Flathead wood screws (3)
#8 x $\frac{1}{2}''$ Panhead screws (2)
#8 x $2''$ Flathead wood screws (30)
$\frac{5}{16}''$ Flat washers (8)
$\frac{1}{4}''$ Flat washers (2)
$\frac{5}{16}''$ Hex nuts (4)
$\frac{1}{4}''$ Wing nuts (2)
$1\frac{1}{2}''$ x $13\frac{1}{2}''$ Piano hinge and
   mounting screws
$1\frac{1}{2}''$ x $2''$ Butt hinges and mounting screws (2)
$2\frac{3}{4}''$ Draw catches and mounting
   screws (2)

Drive train

$\frac{5}{8}''$ I.D. Locking pillow blocks (2)
$\frac{5}{8}''$ dia. x $10''$ Steel shaft
$\frac{5}{8}''$ I.D. x $6''$ O.D. Pulley
$\frac{5}{8}''$ I.D. x $2''$ O.D. Pulley
$37''$ V-belt
$\frac{1}{2}''$ Grinding wheel arbor with right-
   hand threads (for $\frac{5}{8}''$ dia. shaft)

Electrical

$\frac{1}{4}''$-hp, 1,725-rpm, 115-v Motor
   with 56 NEMA frame, clockwise
   rotation at shaft end
Electrical box with cover
Straight cord clamp
Right-angle cord clamp
Grounding plug
14-3 Electrical cord (8')
On/off switch
Terminals (as required)
Cord clips (2 or 3)

PLAN OF PROCEDURE

1 Gather the materials and cut the wooden parts to size. The hollow grinder is essentially a box with a motor inside, powering a drive shaft and a drum mounted on top. The parts of the box are made from $\frac{3}{4}$-inch cabinet-grade plywood — you'll need about a half sheet. You'll also need a quarter sheet of $\frac{1}{2}$-inch medium-density fiberboard (MDF) to make the drum discs and the pulley mounting plate. All the hardware, with the exception of the motor and the pillow blocks, should be readily available at most hardware stores. Have your hardware store special order the motor and pillow blocks; or purchase the motor from an electrical supply house and the pillow blocks from a supplier of bearings and bushings.

When you have gathered all the materials, cut the wooden parts to the sizes given in the Materials List. Miter the back corners of the left side and the top partition at 45 degrees, as shown in the *Left Side Layout* and the *Partition Assembly Layout*. Bevel the adjoining edges of the guard top and back at 45 degrees, as shown in the *Left Side View*.

2 Lay out the shapes, holes, slots, and notches. Lay out the shapes of the following parts (as necessary), as well as the locations of any holes, slots, and notches:

■ The front, as shown in the *Front Layout*
■ The back, as shown in the *Back Layout*
■ The left side, as shown in the *Left Side Layout*
■ The shelf, as shown in the *Shelf Layout*
■ The pulley mounting plate, as shown in the *Pulley Mounting Plate Layout*
■ The motor mount, as shown in the *Motor Mount Layout*
■ The partition top, as shown in the *Partition Assembly Layout*

3 Drill or cut the holes and slots. Drill these holes:

■ A $1\frac{1}{2}$-inch-diameter hole in the center of the pulley mounting plate to accommodate the pulley hub
■ 1-inch-diameter holes in the front and the back to ventilate the motor
■ $\frac{5}{16}$-inch-diameter holes with $\frac{3}{4}$-inch-diameter,

¼-inch-deep counterbores in the motor mount to attach the motor
■ ³⁄₁₆-inch-diameter holes with ½-inch-diameter countersinks in the pulley mounting plate to attach it to the pulley and drum

Then cut out or rout these slots:
■ A 1-inch-wide, 5½-inch-long slot in the shelf to accommodate the V-belt
■ ¼-inch-wide, 6-inch-long slots in the front to mount tool rests

4 Cut the shapes and notches. Using a band saw or a saber saw, cut the notches and any other shapes in the front, back, left side, shelf, partition top, and pulley mounting plate. Sand the cut edges to remove the saw marks.

5 Cut the drum discs. The abrasive drum is made up of ten ½-inch-thick discs glued face to face. To make these, draw the circumferences of the discs on the stock with a compass. Mark the center of each disc, then drill ⅝-inch-diameter holes through the centers of *all* the discs.

Using the ⅝-inch-diameter steel shaft to align the center holes, stack the disc stock face to face, sticking the boards together with double-faced carpet tape. Cut the circumference of the discs with a band saw, sawing the entire stack at once. Make the *Disc Sanding Jig* and use it to sand the stacked discs perfectly round. Refer to *FIGURE 7-1* on page 91 to see how to use this simple jig to round a stack of discs. Take the stack apart and discard the tape.

6 Assemble the grinder housing. Finish sand all the wooden parts. Glue the pillow mounting blocks to the partition bottom and the right side, and the ledger to the back. Let the glue dry, then drill ⁵⁄₁₆-inch-diameter, 1¾-inch-deep holes in the partition bottom and the right side, as shown in the *Pillow Block Mount Detail*.

Using a doweling jig, drill ³⁄₁₆-inch-diameter, ½-inch-deep dowel holes to assemble the partition top and bottom. Glue the parts of the partition together with dowels, let the glue dry, and scrape the glue joint clean and flush.

Assemble the back, sides, bottom, and shelf with glue and flathead wood screws. Then add the partition assembly, guard back, and guard top, attaching them in the same manner. Countersink all screws.

Apply tung oil or Danish oil to all wooden surfaces of the housing assembly, the motor mount, and the

front, inside and out. When the finish dries, fasten the front to the bottom of the assembly with a piano hinge, and secure the front with draw catches.

7 Mount the drum. Using the steel shaft to keep the discs aligned, glue them face to face to make a 5-inch-wide drum. Wipe off any excess glue, then let the drum dry. Don't worry if the surface isn't perfectly smooth; you'll true it later.

TRY THIS TRICK

Spread a little oil or grease on the shaft to prevent it from becoming stuck in the drum.

Loosen the steel shaft and remove it from the drum. File the flats on the shaft as shown in the *Shaft Layout,* then replace the shaft in the drum.

Install the 6-inch-diameter pulley on the shaft so it butts against the right side of the drum, and place the pulley mounting plate over it. Using the holes in the plate as a guide, drill ³⁄₁₆-inch-diameter holes through the pulley. Fasten the pulley and the pulley mounting plate to the drum with #12 flathead wood screws, but don't tighten the locking screw that secures the pulley to the shaft.

Insert the ends of the shaft through the pillow blocks, and tighten the locking screws on the *right* pillow block. The right end of the shaft should protrude about ⅛ inch from the right pillow block. Position the drum assembly in the grinder housing so the right pillow block is over the holes in the right side. Adjust the position of the drum so it doesn't rub on any part of the grinder; adjust the left pillow block so it's over the holes in the partition. Tighten the locking screws in the pulley and the left pillow block.

Secure the pillow blocks to the housing with lag screws. Fasten a grinding wheel arbor to the left end of the shaft.

8 Install the motor. Decide where you want to install the switch on the grinder. As shown, it's on the left side, near the bottom. However, you may prefer to mount it somewhere else. Mark the position of the electrical switch box on the grinder, and drill a 1-inch-diameter hole next to it to run the wiring. Install a right-angle cord clamp and a straight cord clamp in the electrical box. Attach the box to the grinder with #8 panhead screws so the right-angle cord clamp is inserted in the 1-inch-diameter hole.

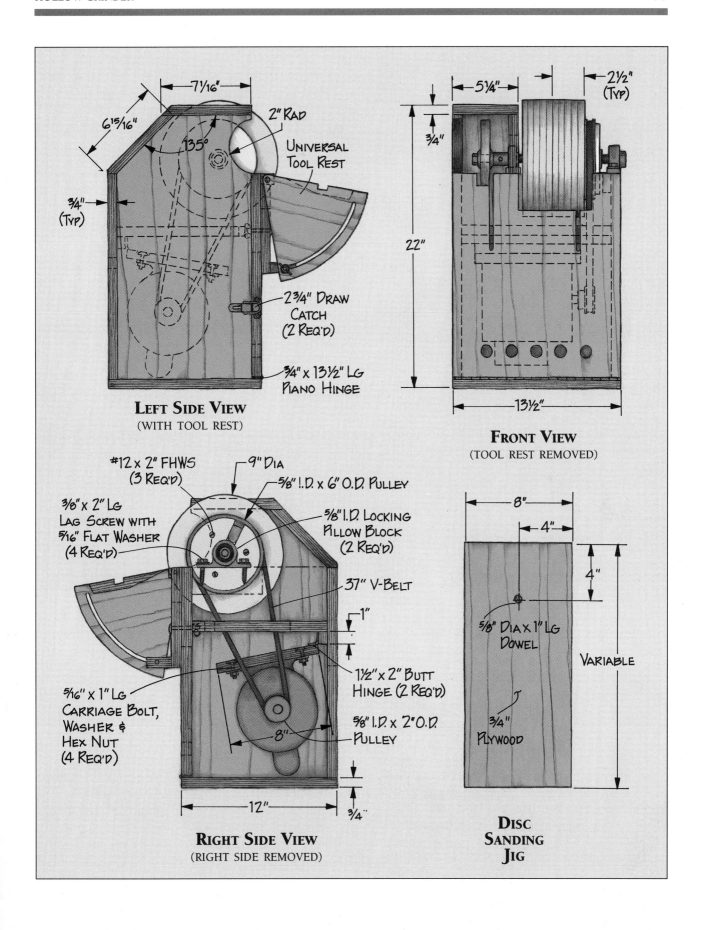

LEFT SIDE VIEW
(WITH TOOL REST)

7¹/₁₆"

6¹⁵/₁₆"

135°

2" RAD

UNIVERSAL
TOOL REST

¾"
(TYP)

2¾" DRAW
CATCH
(2 REQ'D)

¾" x 13½" LG
PIANO HINGE

FRONT VIEW
(TOOL REST REMOVED)

5¼"

2½"
(TYP)

¾"

22"

13½"

RIGHT SIDE VIEW
(RIGHT SIDE REMOVED)

#12 x 2" FHWS
(3 REQ'D)

9" DIA

5/8" I.D. x 6" O.D. PULLEY

3/8" x 2" LG
LAG SCREW WITH
5/16" FLAT WASHER
(4 REQ'D)

5/8" I.D. LOCKING
PILLOW BLOCK
(2 REQ'D)

37" V-BELT

1"

1½" x 2" BUTT
HINGE (2 REQ'D)

5/16" x 1" LG
CARRIAGE BOLT,
WASHER &
HEX NUT
(4 REQ'D)

8"

5/8" I.D. x 2" O.D.
PULLEY

12"

¾"

**DISC
SANDING
JIG**

8"

4"

4"

5/8" DIA x 1" LG
DOWEL

VARIABLE

¾"

PLYWOOD

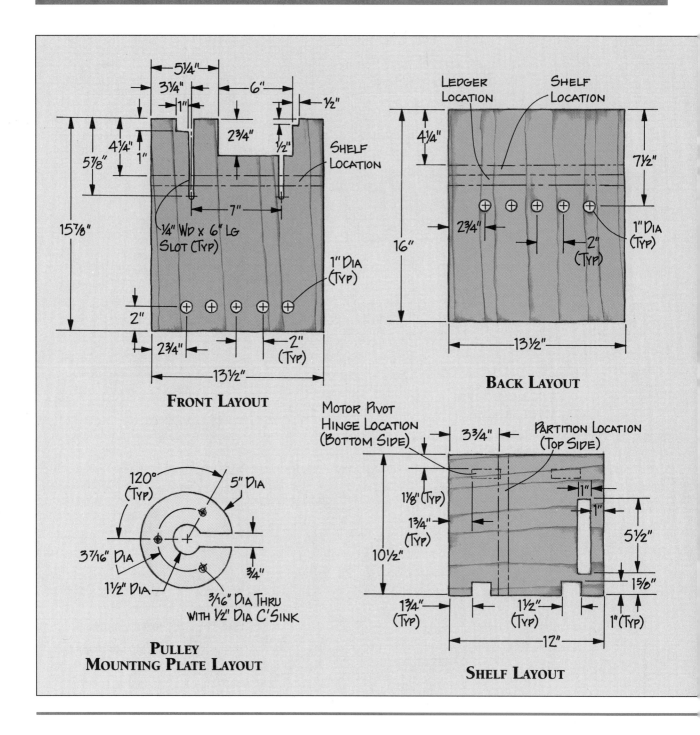

FRONT LAYOUT

BACK LAYOUT

**PULLEY
MOUNTING PLATE LAYOUT**

SHELF LAYOUT

Attach one end of the electrical cord to the motor using terminals. Run the cord to the electrical box and pull all but 1½ feet of the cord through the right-angle clamp. Carefully pare away the plastic covering from a 3-inch-long section of cord just inside the box. Snip the line (black) wire *only* in two, strip away the insulation from the ends, and attach the cut ends to a switch.

Run the free end of the cord out of the electrical box through the straight cord clamp. Attach the switch to the electrical box, then attach the box cover. Install a grounded plug on the free end of the cord. Use cord clips to fasten the portion of the cord inside the grinder to the housing.

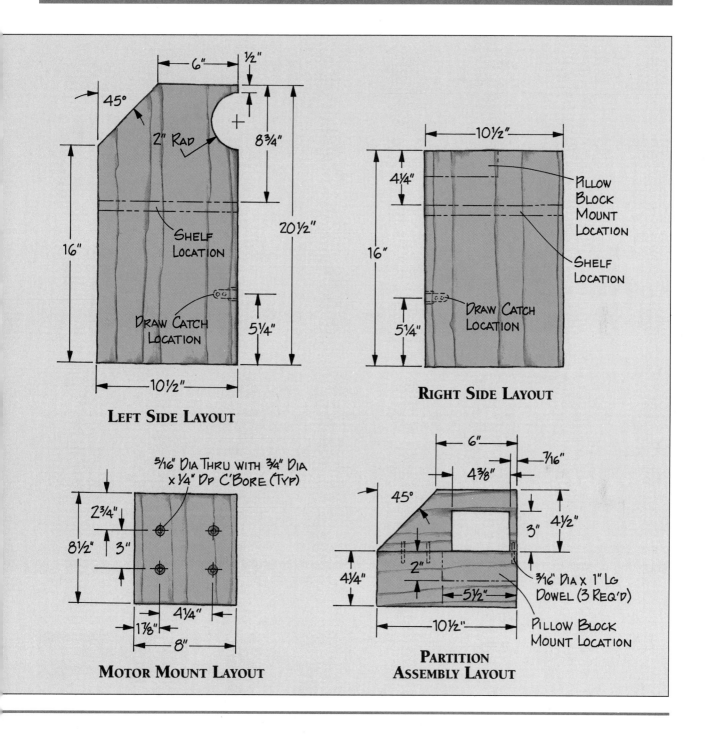

LEFT SIDE LAYOUT

RIGHT SIDE LAYOUT

MOTOR MOUNT LAYOUT

PARTITION ASSEMBLY LAYOUT

Attach the butt hinges to the motor mount, near the back edge. Mark the locations of the hinges on the ledger and drill pilot holes for the mounting screws, but don't fasten the hinges to the ledger yet. Fasten the motor to the motor mount with 5/16-inch carriage bolts and install a 2-inch pulley on the motor arbor. Then attach the motor mount inside the housing, screwing the butt hinges to the ledger.

Swing the motor up and loop the V-belt over the pulleys. Then let the motor swing down — its weight will tension the belt. Turn on the motor and make sure the drum rotates *up* as you face the front. If not, you'll have to remove the motor and follow the directions on the label to reverse the rotation.

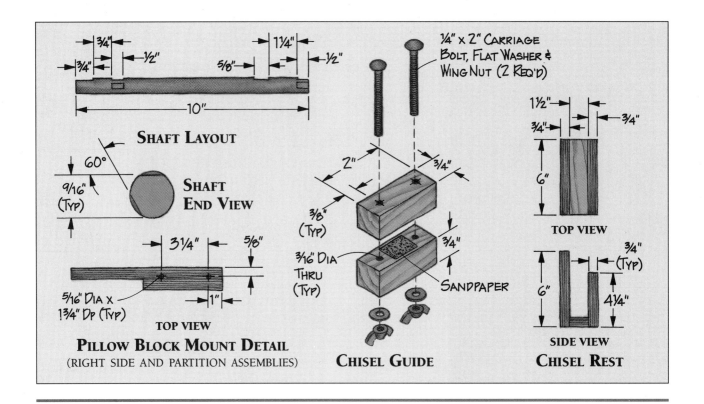

SHAFT LAYOUT

SHAFT END VIEW

PILLOW BLOCK MOUNT DETAIL
(RIGHT SIDE AND PARTITION ASSEMBLIES)

CHISEL GUIDE

¼" x 2" CARRIAGE BOLT, FLAT WASHER & WING NUT (2 REQ'D)

SANDPAPER

CHISEL REST

TOP VIEW

SIDE VIEW

9 **True the drum.** Make the temporary *Chisel Rest* and *Chisel Guide* from scraps of ³/₄-inch plywood. Clamp the chisel rest to the housing, behind the drum. Turn on the motor to start the drum, and carefully scrape away the rough surface with a lathe chisel. Then clamp the chisel guide to a flatnose chisel. Using the guide and the rest to control the chisel, cut the surface of the drum perfectly round and true. *(SEE FIGURE 8-1.)*

Once the drum is true, lightly sand it and coat it with white shellac.

10 **Mount the abrasive on the drum.** Decide what abrasive grades you want to use with your hollow grinder. (I suggest 120- and 320-grit aluminum oxide.) Purchase the abrasives in rolls, and cut off 2¹/₂-inch-wide, 30-inch-long strips. Apply a spray adhesive to the drum and the back of each abrasive strip. Wrap the abrasive around the drum so it laps over itself, then trim the ends diagonally with a utility knife. *(SEE FIGURE 8-2.)*

8-1 To true the drum, first clamp the chisel rest to the housing, behind the drum, and fasten the chisel guide to a flatnose chisel. Adjust the position of the guide so the chisel will just barely cut the drum when you hold the guide against the edge of the rest. Turn on the grinder and draw the chisel slowly across the surface, keeping the guide pressed firmly against the rest. If there are any areas of the drum that haven't been cut, readjust the chisel guide so the chisel will go about ¹/₆₄ inch deeper, and cut again. Repeat until the entire drum has been cut round and true.

8-2 Stick 2½-inch-wide, 30-inch-long abrasive strips to the drum with spray adhesive. Lap the ends of each strip over one another and draw them as tight as possible. Where the ends lap, cut across the strip diagonally with a utility knife. Cut all the way through both layers of the abrasive. Peel the ends back partially, remove the waste, and press them back in place. The cut ends will butt together perfectly.

USING THE HOLLOW GRINDER

The hollow grinder can perform the same sharpening tasks as a bench grinder and a buffing head. Use it to hollow grind chisel and plane irons before sharpening them and to buff the cutting edges after they've been sharpened.

1 **Use a tool rest to maintain** a precise angle as you hollow grind. The universal tool rest shown mounts in the slots in the front. By itself, it will handle most flat chisels and plane irons. Add guide blocks for skew chisels, gouges, and V-tools. (Plans for this tool rest are on page 104.) You can also devise your own tool rests and mount them in the same slots.

2 **The arbor on the left end of** the shaft is a good place to mount a buffing wheel — this lets you grind and buff on the same machine. To mount a buffing wheel, loosen the locking screws that hold the arbor to the shaft. Remove the arbor, mount a wheel on it, then replace the arbor on the shaft.

UNIVERSAL TOOL REST

This simple tool rest offers a large work surface to support the tools and to mount guide blocks when sharpening complex cutting edges. It tilts through a full 65 degrees, allowing you to grind every common tool angle from 15 to 80 degrees. It's designed to work with both the flat grinder (page 86) and the hollow grinder (page 95). You can also adapt this design for use with some commercial sharpening machines and sanders.

1 **To make the tool rest, rout** two identical curved slots, one in each trunnion. Cut the shapes of the trunnions and drill $^3/_{16}$-inch-diameter pivot holes in them. Also drill $^1/_4$-inch-diameter holes to mark the ends of each slot. Fasten one trunnion to the jig, driving a #8 flathead screw through the pivot hole, then push it sideways against the right stop. Mount a $^1/_4$-inch-diameter straight bit in a table-mounted router, and clamp the jig to the router table so the left slot-end hole is directly above the router bit. Adjust the depth of cut so the bit will rout about $^1/_8$ inch in the trunnion. Turn on the router and swing the trunnion slowly to the left. Turn off the router, adjust the router to take another $^1/_8$-inch bite, and rout again. Repeat until you have routed the slot completely though the trunnion. Then do the same for the other trunnion.

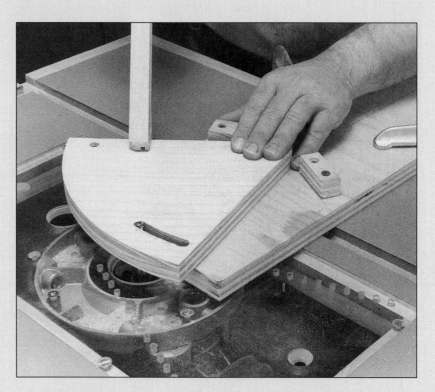

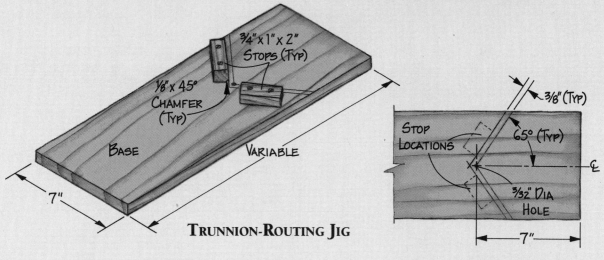

TRUNNION-ROUTING JIG

$^3/_4$" x 1" x 2" STOPS (TYP)

$^1/_8$" x 45° CHAMFER (TYP)

BASE

VARIABLE

7"

STOP AND PIVOT LAYOUT

STOP LOCATIONS

$^3/_8$" (TYP)

65° (TYP)

$^3/_{32}$" DIA HOLE

7"

2 **To mount the universal tool** rest on either the flat grinder or the hollow grinder, simply slide the carriage bolts into the mounting slots and tighten the wing nuts. Adjust the rest to the desired angle and lock it in place. Lay the blade of the chisel on the removable ledger, turn on the grinder, and gently feed the cutting edge into the moving abrasive.

3 **To sharpen or hollow grind** tools with complex cutting edges — skew chisels, gouges, and V-tools — remove the ledger from the rest and replace it with special guide blocks. Here, a guide block with a V-groove is being used to hollow grind a gouge.

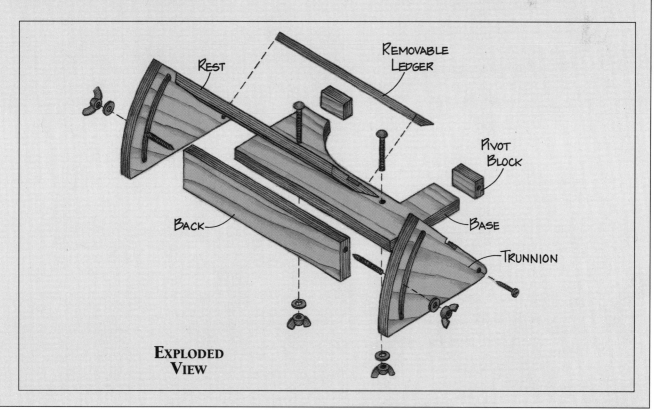

REST

REMOVABLE LEDGER

PIVOT BLOCK

BACK

BASE

TRUNNION

EXPLODED VIEW

(continued) ▷

Universal Tool Rest — continued

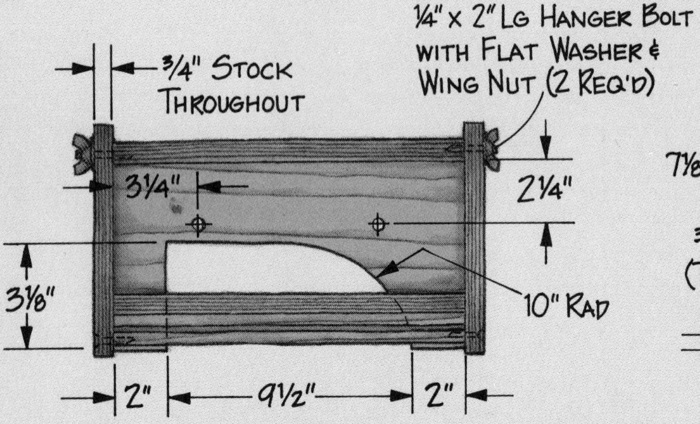
3/4" Stock Throughout
1/4" x 2" Lg Hanger Bolt with Flat Washer & Wing Nut (2 Req'd)
3 1/4"
2 1/4"
3 1/8"
10" Rad
2"
9 1/2"
2"

Top View

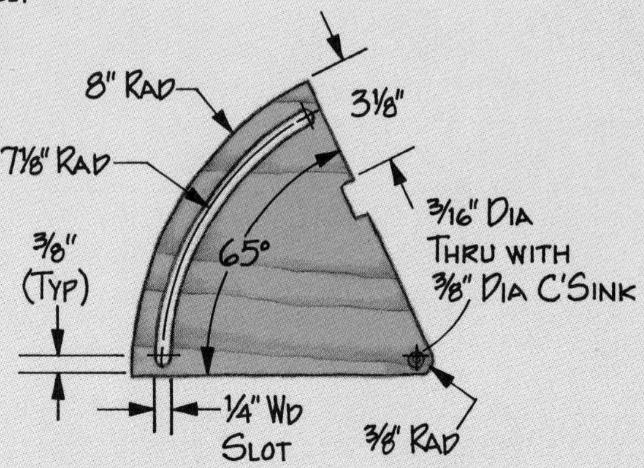
8" Rad
3 1/8"
7 1/8" Rad
3/16" Dia Thru with 3/8" Dia C'Sink
3/8" (Typ)
65°
1/4" Wd Slot
3/8" Rad

Trunnion Layout

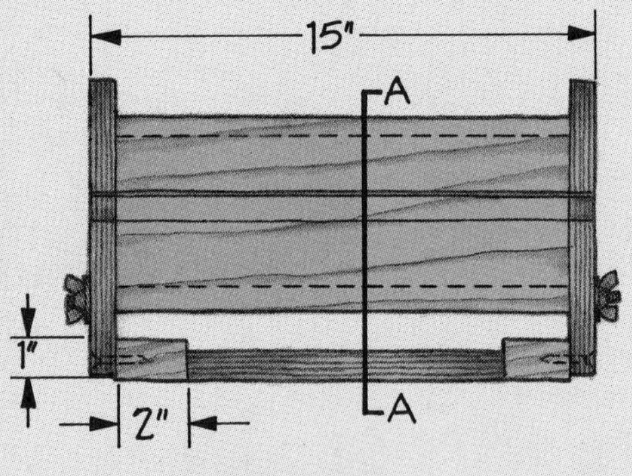
15"
A
1"
2"
A

Front View

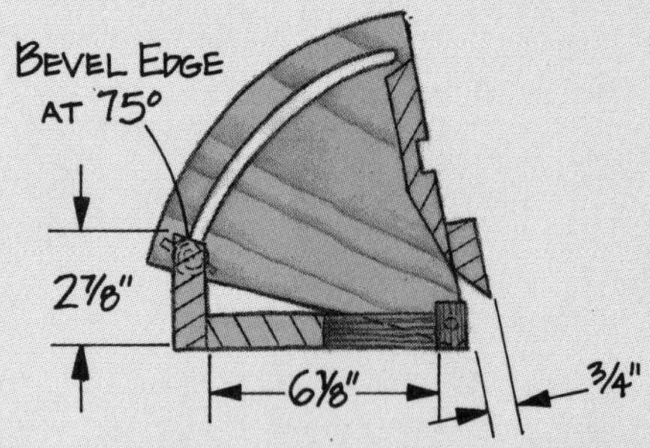
Bevel Edge at 75°
2 7/8"
6 1/8"
3/4"

Section A

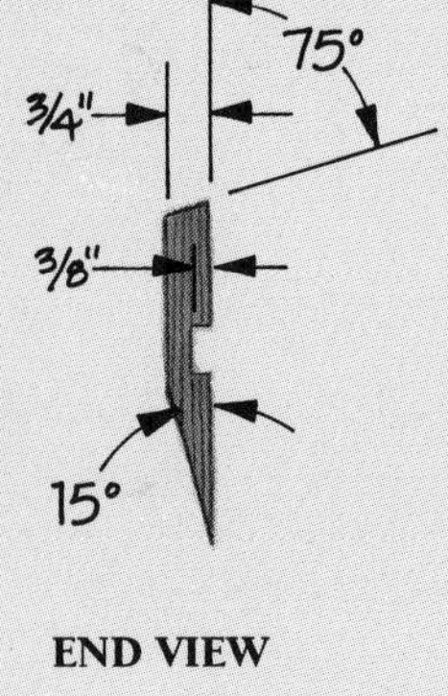
75°
3/4"
3/8"
15°

END VIEW

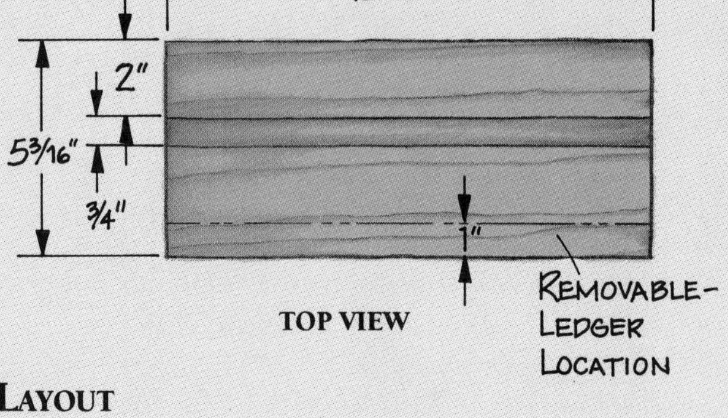
13 1/2"
2"
5 3/16"
3/4"
1"
Removable-Ledger Location

TOP VIEW

Rest Layout

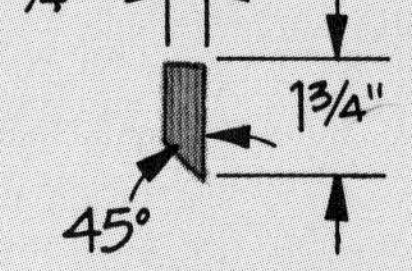
3/4"
1 3/4"
45°

Removable-Ledger Detail

NOTE: Fasten the ledger to the rest with screws only.

9

STRIP SANDER SHARPENING SYSTEM

Don't be misled by the simplicity of this setup. An ordinary strip sander, combined with this shopmade fixture, is one of the most versatile sharpening machines in this book. It's also the easiest to use, bar none.

The secret of its usefulness is the unusual way in which the fixture supports the chisel. Clamp the *handle* (not the blade) in the holder, place the holder on the rest, then lean the cutting edge against the abrasive belt. The rest adjusts to accommodate the length of the chisel and the tool angle. The fixture keeps the tool at a precise angle to the belt *and* allows you to roll or rotate the tool as you work. You can sharpen flat chisels, skews, gouges, and V-tools with equal ease *without using special guide blocks!* The one drawback is that you can only sharpen tools as wide as the belt — the fixture will not work for chisels or plane irons wider than 1 inch.

Note: This system will work with almost any strip sander, provided it can accommodate the belt backup. The backup assembly is extremely important; it keeps the belt perfectly flat so you can grind a flat surface.

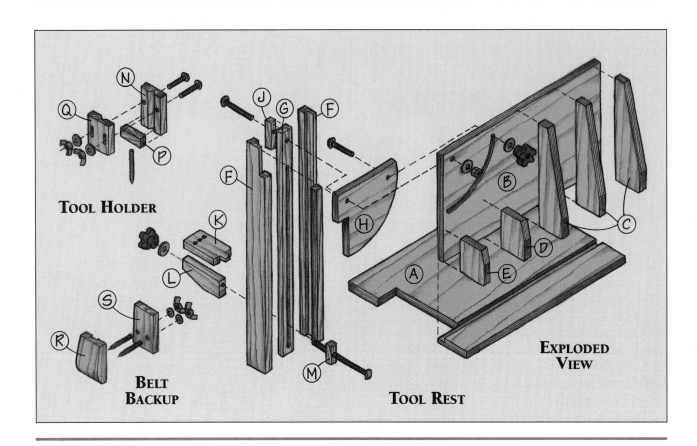

TOOL HOLDER

BELT BACKUP

TOOL REST

EXPLODED VIEW

MATERIALS LIST (FINISHED DIMENSIONS)

Parts

Tool Rest

A.	Base*	³/₄″ x 14³/₄″ x 20″
B.	Support*	³/₄″ x 11³/₈″ x 20″
C.	Long braces* (3)	³/₄″ x 3″ x 11″
D.	Medium brace*	³/₄″ x 3″ x 4³/₄″
E.	Short brace*	³/₄″ x 3″ x 3¹/₂″
F.	Stiffeners (2)	³/₄″ x 2¹/₄″ x 24″
G.	Arm	³/₄″ x 1¹/₂″ x 24″
H.	Trunnion*	³/₄″ x 7″ x 7¹/₈″
J.	Spacer	³/₄″ x ³/₄″ x 3″
K.	Rest	³/₄″ x 2¹/₄″ x 4³/₄″
L.	Rest brace	³/₄″ x 1³/₄″ x 4³/₄″
M.	Slide	¹/₂″ x ³/₄″ x 1³/₄″

Tool Holder

N.	Holder	³/₄″ x 2¹/₂″ x 4″
P.	Pivot block	³/₄″ x 1″ x 2¹/₂″
Q.	Tool clamp	³/₄″ x 2¹/₂″ x 3″

Belt Backup

R.	Backup block	1″ x 2¹/₂″ x 4″
S.	Backup clamp	³/₄″ x 2¹/₂″ x 4″

Hardware

Tool Rest

#8 x 2″ Flathead wood screws (18–24)
³/₈″ x 7″ Carriage bolt
³/₈″ x 3¹/₂″ Carriage bolt
³/₈″ x 2″ Carriage bolt
³/₈″ Flat washers (3)
³/₈″ Stop nut
³/₈″ Threaded star knobs (2)

Tool Holder

¹/₄″ x 3″ Carriage bolts (2)
¹/₄″ Flat washers (2)
¹/₄″ Wing nuts (2)
¹/₄″ dia. x 2³/₄″ Steel pin

Belt Backup

¹/₄″ x 2″ Hanger bolts (2)
¹/₄″ Flat washers (2)
¹/₄″ Wing nuts (2)

Make these parts from plywood.

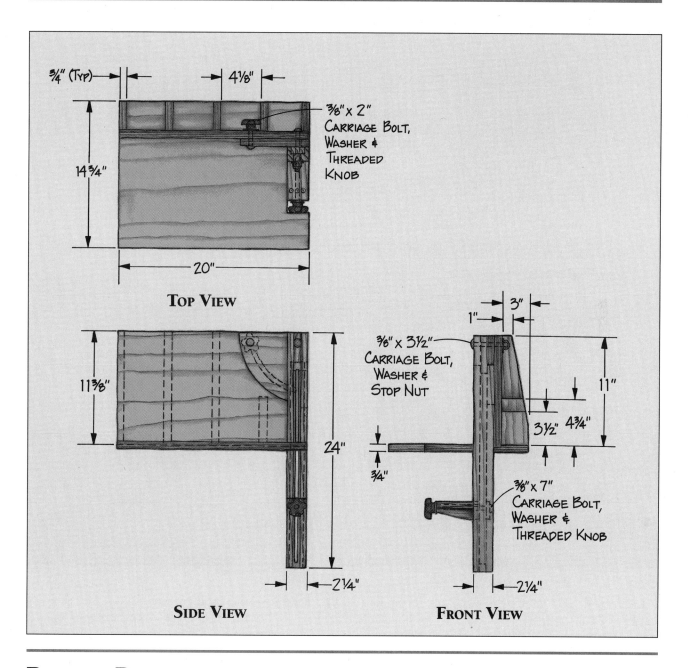

TOP VIEW

SIDE VIEW

FRONT VIEW

PLAN OF PROCEDURE

1 Gather the materials and cut the parts to size.
To make this fixture, you need about 2 board feet of a 4/4 (four-quarter) hardwood and a quarter sheet of ³/₄-inch cabinet-grade plywood. Choose a dense, closed-grain hardwood such as maple or birch. If you prefer, you can use Baltic birch or Apple-ply plywood to make everything but the backup block. These materials are slightly stronger and much more stable than ordinary plywood. The sharpening jig shown is made from Baltic birch plywood and hard maple.

Plane the 4/4 stock to ³/₄ inch thick. Cut the parts to the sizes given in the Materials List, except for the backup block. For this part, cut two pieces of ³/₄-inch-thick hardwood, 2¹/₂ inches wide and 4 inches long, and glue them face to face to make a single 1¹/₂-inch-thick block. Later, you'll cut the backup block from this glued-up piece.

2 Lay out the shapes and joinery. Lay out the shapes, holes, notches, dadoes, grooves, slots, and

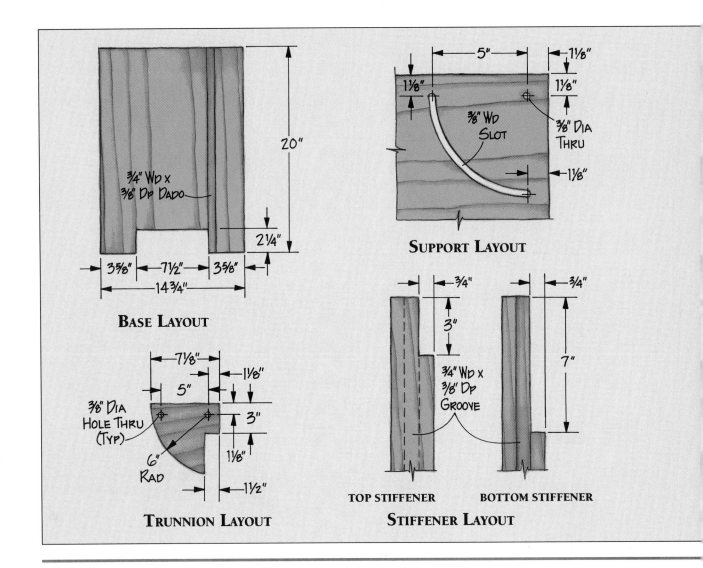

BASE LAYOUT

SUPPORT LAYOUT

TRUNNION LAYOUT

STIFFENER LAYOUT

other characteristics on the following parts according to the working drawings:

- The base, as shown in the *Base Layout*
- The support, as shown in the *Support Layout*
- The trunnion, as shown in the *Trunnion Layout*
- The stiffeners, as shown in the *Stiffener Layout*
- The arm, as shown in the *Arm Assembly/Side View*
- The rest, as shown in the *Rest Assembly/Top View*
- The rest brace, as shown in the *Rest Assembly/Front View*
- The holder, as shown in the *Tool Holder/Top View* and *Tool Holder/Side View*
- The tool clamp and pivot block, as shown in the *Tool Holder/Front View*
- The backup block and backup clamp, as shown in the *Belt Backup/Side View*

3 Drill the holes and countersinks. You can't drill all the holes now — a few of them must wait until you assemble the fixture — but you can drill the following:

- Three ³⁄₈-inch-diameter holes in the support — one to serve as a pivot hole and the other two to mark the ends of the curved slot
- ³⁄₈-inch-diameter holes to mark the ends of the slot in the arm
- ³⁄₈-inch-diameter holes through the length of the rest brace and the face of the slide
- ¹⁄₄-inch-diameter holes in the holder
- A ¹⁄₄-inch-diameter, ³⁄₄-inch-deep hole in the pivot block
- ¹⁄₄-inch-diameter holes in the backup clamp
- ³⁄₁₆-inch-diameter pilot holes for the hanger bolts in the backup block

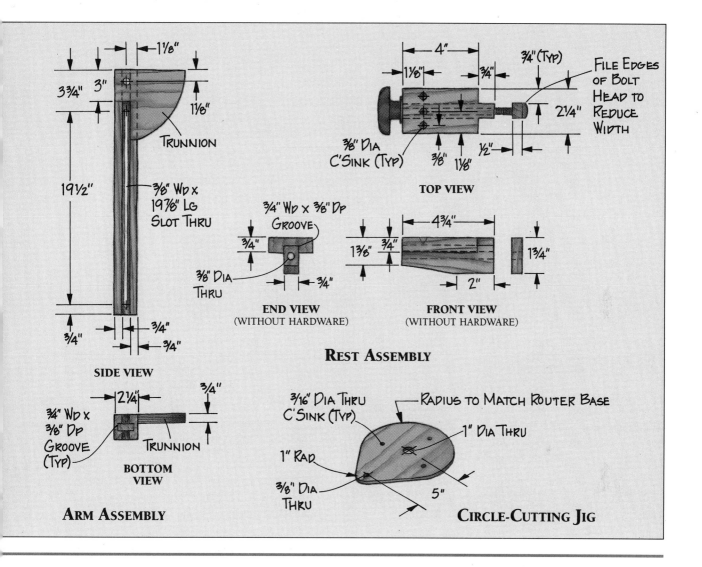

SIDE VIEW

END VIEW
(WITHOUT HARDWARE)

FRONT VIEW
(WITHOUT HARDWARE)

TOP VIEW

REST ASSEMBLY

BOTTOM VIEW

ARM ASSEMBLY

CIRCLE-CUTTING JIG

Also drill the ⅜-inch-diameter countersinks in the rest to hold the pointed end of the tool holder.

4 Cut the grooves and dadoes. Portions of the jig are assembled with grooves or dadoes. Using a router or a dado cutter, make a shallow groove in the back face of the backup block. This groove must be slightly wider than the platen on the strip sander and not quite as deep as the platen's thickness. Also make these joints:

■ A ¾-inch-wide, ⅜-inch-deep dado in the base to hold the support

■ ¾-inch-wide, ⅜-inch-deep grooves in the stiffeners to hold the slotted arm

■ A ¾-inch-wide, ⅜-inch-deep groove in the rest to hold the rest brace

Cut the ⅞-inch-wide V-grooves in the holder and tool clamp on a table saw with an ordinary saw blade. Tilt the blade to 45 degrees. Make one pass to cut one side of each groove; turn the part around and make a second pass to cut the other side.

A SAFETY REMINDER

To cut small parts safely on a table saw, attach them to a push block with double-faced carpet tape.

5 Rout the slots. Rout the ⅜-inch-wide, 19⅞-inch-long slot in the arm on a table-mounted router using a straight bit. To make the curved slot in the

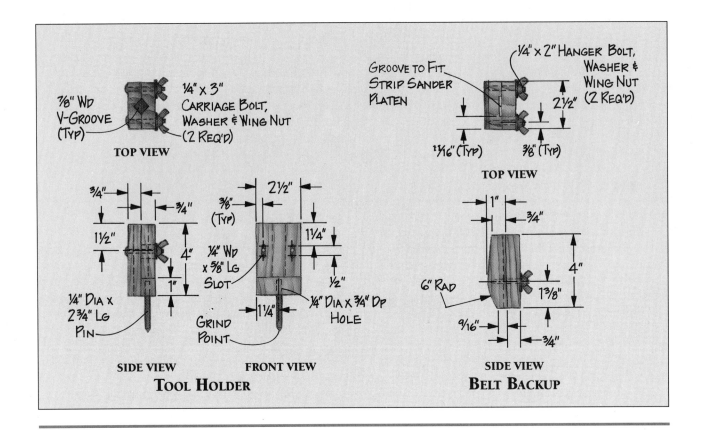

TOOL HOLDER

BELT BACKUP

support, attach the support to the *Circle-Cutting Jig* and use the jig to guide the router. (SEE FIGURE 9-1.)

To make the 1/4-inch-wide, 5/8-inch-long slots in the tool clamp, drill a series of overlapping 1/4-inch-diameter holes. (SEE FIGURE 9-2.)

6 Cut the shapes. Using a band saw or a saber saw, cut the shapes of the base, trunnion, stiffeners, rest, rest brace, and backup block. Stack the long, medium, and short braces face to face with the shortest braces toward the top of the stack. Stick the braces together with double-faced carpet tape so the sides and the bottom ends are flush. Then cut the taper in the entire stack.

Sand the cut surfaces to remove the saw marks. As you sand the backup block, make the top two-thirds of the front face *perfectly flat*. Only the bottom third should be rounded. When you've finished sanding all the parts, take the stacked braces apart and discard the tape.

7 Assemble the tool rest. Finish sand all the parts. Glue the base, support, and braces together, then reinforce the assembly with flathead wood screws. Counterbore and countersink the screws.

Cover the screw heads with wooden plugs and sand the plugs flush with the surrounding surfaces.

Glue the trunnion, arm, stiffeners, and spacer together. Let the glue dry, then sand the glue joints clean and flush. Clamp the arm assembly to the support so the top and the front edges are flush. Using the pivot hole in the support as a guide, drill a 3/8-inch-diameter pivot hole through the trunnion, arm, and spacer. Also drill a hole through the trunnion only, using the top end of the curved slot to guide the drill bit. Insert a 3 1/2-inch-long carriage bolt through the pivot holes, and secure it with a washer and a stop nut. Insert a 2-inch-long carriage bolt through the trunnion and the curved slot, and secure it with a washer and a threaded star knob. **Note:** You can substitute wing nuts for the threaded knobs, if you wish.

Glue the rest to the rest brace. While the glue dries, file the head of a 7-inch-long carriage bolt to fit in the recesses in the arm. (The head must be less than 3/4 inch wide.) Test the slide and the rest assembly to make sure they slip up and down the arm recesses. If they bind, file or sand away a little stock until they move smoothly. Secure them to the arm with the long carriage bolt, a flat washer, and a threaded knob, as shown in the *Front View*.

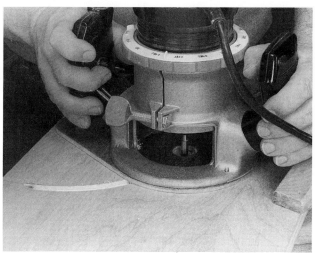

9-1 To rout the curved slot in the support, mount a $^3/_8$-inch-diameter straight bit in your router and attach the *Circle-Cutting Jig* to the base. Fasten the jig to the support, inserting a $^3/_8$-inch carriage bolt through the pivot holes in both pieces. Position the router above one of the holes that marks an end of the slot. Adjust the depth of cut, lowering the bit approximately $^1/_8$ inch into the hole. Turn on the router and cut until you reach the other hole, pivoting the tool around the carriage bolt. Readjust the depth of cut to take another $^1/_8$-inch bite and repeat. Continue until you rout the slot through the support.

1 | DRILL OVER-LAPPING HOLES
2 | WORK BIT BACK AND FORTH

9-2 To rough out each slot in the tool clamp, drill a series of overlapping $^1/_4$-inch-diameter holes. Then work the drill bit back and forth in the rough slot to remove the remaining waste.

8 Assemble the tool holder. Glue the pivot block to the holder. Grind a point on one end of a $^1/_4$-inch-diameter, $2^3/_4$-inch-long steel pin. (*SEE FIGURE 9-3.*) Secure the blunt end in the stopped hole in the pivot block with epoxy cement. Fasten the tool clamp to the holder with $^1/_4$-inch carriage bolts, washers, and wing nuts.

9 Assemble the belt backup. Install the hanger bolts in the backup block on either side of the groove. Secure the backup clamp to the block with washers and wing nuts. Check that the assembly fits over the strip sander platen.

10 Finish the fixture. Remove the arm assembly from the support and the clamps from the tool holder and belt backup. Set the hardware aside and finish sand the wooden surfaces. Apply several coats of tung oil or Danish oil, letting the finish dry thoroughly between each coat. Rub out the last coat with #0000 steel wool and paste wax — the wax will help the moving parts of the fixture work smoothly. Reassemble the tool rest, tool holder, and belt backup.

9-3 To grind a symmetrical point on the end of the steel pin, mount it in the chuck of a portable electric drill. Mount a coarse abrasive on a belt sander or a disc sander and turn on both the sander and the drill. Place the end of the steel pin against the abrasive so the pin rotates in the opposite direction of the abrasive. Hold the pin steady at a 30- to 45-degree angle to the sander until a point develops. **Note:** The angle of the point must be more acute than the angle of the countersink you used to make the depressions in the rest.

USING THE STRIP SANDER SHARPENING SYSTEM

Make sure that the abrasive belt on your strip sander travels at 1,600 fpm or less. As they come from the factory, most sanders run faster than this, but you usually can adjust them to run at the proper sharpening speed by installing a drive pulley that's the same size as the motor pulley. If you want to use a leather belt on your strip sander to buff tools, change the motor rotation so the belt travels *up* as you face the front of the machine.

Remove the table from the sander and install the belt backup on the platen. On some machines, you may have to modify the belt guard or make a new one to accommodate the backup block. *Don't use the machine without a belt guard.*

1 **Clamp the handle of the** chisel you want to sharpen in the tool holder. The clamp will accommodate almost any common size and shape of handle.

2 **Place the pointed end of the** holder pin in the tool rest countersink closest to the sander. Adjust the position of the rest on the arm so the cutting edge meets the abrasive belt over the flat area on the belt backup. Tilt the arm to hold the chisel at the proper angle. Turn on the sander and lightly touch the bevel to the belt. If you're sharpening a skew, gouge, or V-tool, roll or rotate the tool as needed. Grind the bevel with a 120-grit belt, hone with 320-grit, and polish with 600-grit. *Don't move the arm, the rest, or the sander when you change belts.* Keep the setup exactly the same to maintain the proper tool angle as you work your way through finer and finer abrasives.

Place the sander on the base of the fixture and position it so the protruding surface of the belt backup is about even with or just behind the arm pivot. (It doesn't matter if the belt backup is above or below the pivot.) The sander must be perfectly stationary as you work. If the machine isn't heavy enough to stay put, bolt it to the base.

WHERE TO FIND IT

You can purchase leather stropping belts and fine abrasive belts for sharpening from:

Woodworker's Supply
1108 North Glenn Road
Casper, WY 82601

3 **To sharpen the back of the** chisel, use a bench stone, slip stone, or gouge slip. You may wish to place a set of stones next to the sander so you can easily switch between the two sharpening tools. *Don't* remove the chisel from the holder when you use the stones — keep it attached so you always maintain the same tool angle when you go back to the sander.

4 **To buff the bevel, use a** leather belt and buffing compound. You can run abrasive belts in either direction, but *leather belts must travel up* as you face the sander or the cutting edge will dig into them. If you want to put a microbevel on the cutting edge, wait until you've finished polishing or buffing the bevel. Then move the point of the holder toward you, to the middle or foremost countersink, and touch the tip of the tool to the belt *for just a moment*.

10

Sharpening Station

Sharpening and touching up all the cutting tools in your shop require several pieces of equipment and a good many materials — bench stones, slip stones, files, strops, buffing compounds, honing guides, guide blocks, and so on. To store and use them all, you need a sharpening station.

This easy-to-build storage stand is the right height to hold a motorized whetstone, the flat grinder, or the hollow grinder at a comfortable working level. The optional shelving unit will hold a bench grinder, a buffing head, or the strip sander sharpening system where you can reach it easily. And there's plenty of storage space for sharpening materials in the drawers or on the shelves.

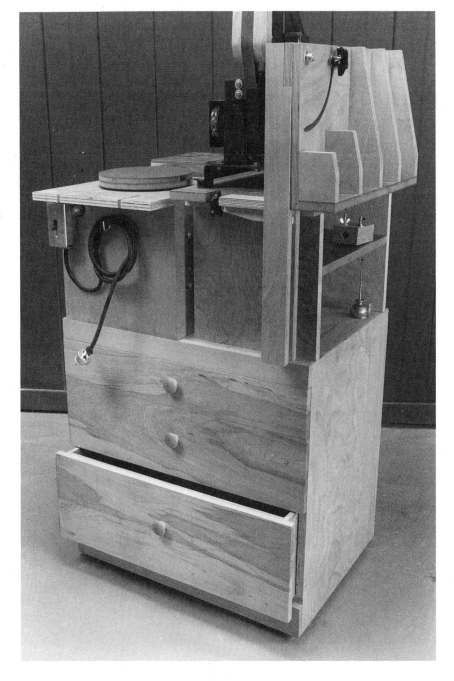

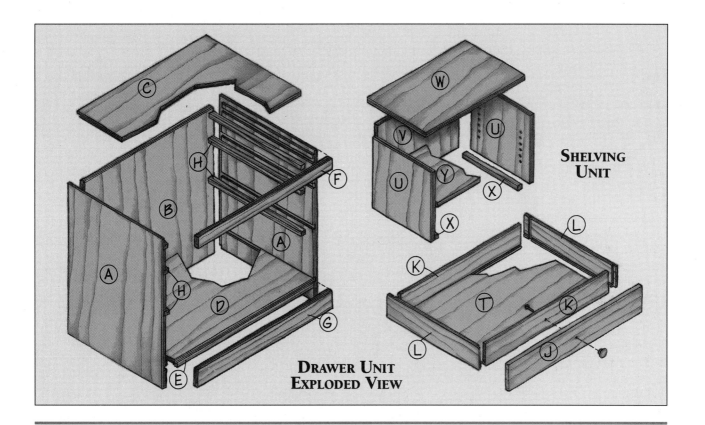

DRAWER UNIT EXPLODED VIEW

SHELVING UNIT

MATERIALS LIST (FINISHED DIMENSIONS)

Parts

Drawer Unit

A. Sides* (2)   3/4" x 19¼" x 25¼"
B. Back*   3/4" x 24⅞" x 26¼"
C. Top*   3/4" x 19¼" x 26¼"
D. Shelf*   3/4" x 18½" x 26¼"
E. Cleat   3/4" x 3/4" x 25½"
F. Valance   3/4" x 2" x 27"
G. Apron   3/4" x 2⅝" x 27"
H. Drawer guides (6)   3/4" x 1" x 18½"
J. Top drawer face   3/4" x 4⁷/₁₆" x 27"
K. Top drawer front/ back* (2)   ½" x 3⅝" x 24⅞"
L. Top drawer sides* (2)   ½" x 3⅝" x 18¼"
M. Middle drawer face   3/4" x 6¹⁵/₁₆" x 27"
N. Middle drawer front/ back* (2)   ½" x 6⅛" x 24⅞"
P. Middle drawer sides* (2)   ½" x 6⅛" x 18¼"

Q. Bottom drawer face   3/4" x 9¹/₁₆" x 27"
R. Bottom drawer front/ back* (2)   ½" x 8¼" x 24⅞"
S. Bottom drawer sides* (2)   ½" x 8¼" x 18¼"
T. Drawer bottoms* (3)   ¼" x 16⅞" x 24⅞"

Shelving Unit

U. Shelving sides* (2)   3/4" x 12" x 12"
V. Shelving back*   3/4" x 12" x 16½"
W. Shelving top*   3/4" x 12" x 20"
X. Shelving cleats (2)   3/4" x 3/4" x 11¼"
Y. Adjustable shelf   3/4" x 11⅛" x 16⅜"

Make these parts from plywood.

Hardware

Drawer Unit

#8 Flathead wood screws (36–42)
1" Wire brads (36–42)
2" Drawer pulls (3)
4" Casters and mounting screws (4)

Shelving Unit

#8 Flathead wood screws (18–24)
Shelving support pins (4)

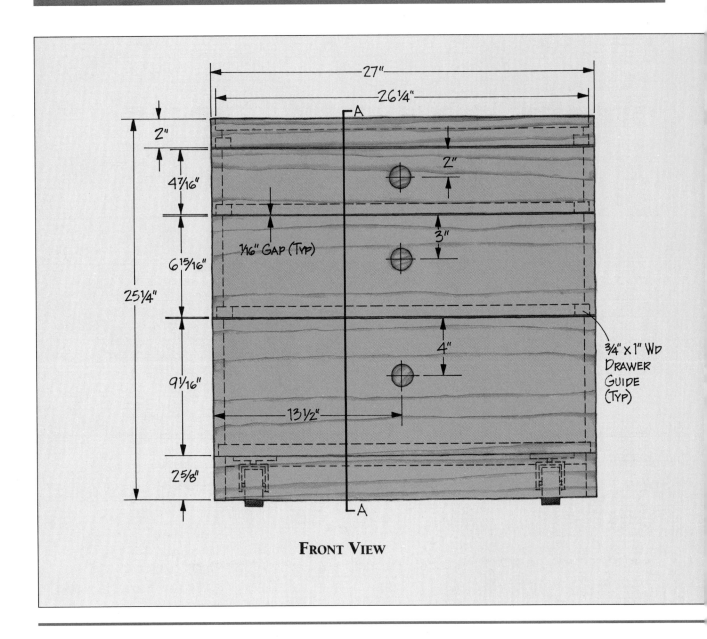

FRONT VIEW

PLAN OF PROCEDURE

1 **Select the stock and cut the parts to size.**
To make the drawer unit, you'll need about 6 board feet of 4/4 (four-quarter) hardwood stock, two-thirds sheet of 3/4-inch cabinet-grade plywood, one-quarter sheet of 1/2-inch plywood, and one-quarter sheet of 1/4-inch plywood. The shelving unit requires another board foot of 4/4 hardwood and an additional one-third sheet of 3/4-inch plywood. (You can make both units from a full sheet.) The type of hardwood doesn't matter, as long as it's durable and matches the plywood veneer. The sharpening station shown was made from hard maple and birch-veneered plywood.

Plane the 4/4 stock to 3/4 inch thick, then cut the parts to the sizes given in the Materials List, except the drawer parts. Wait until after you've built the case to cut these.

MAKING THE DRAWER UNIT

2 **Cut the joinery in the sides and top.** The parts of the drawer unit case are assembled with rabbets and dadoes. Cut these joints, using a router or a dado cutter:
■ 3/4-inch-wide, 3/8-inch-deep rabbets in the back

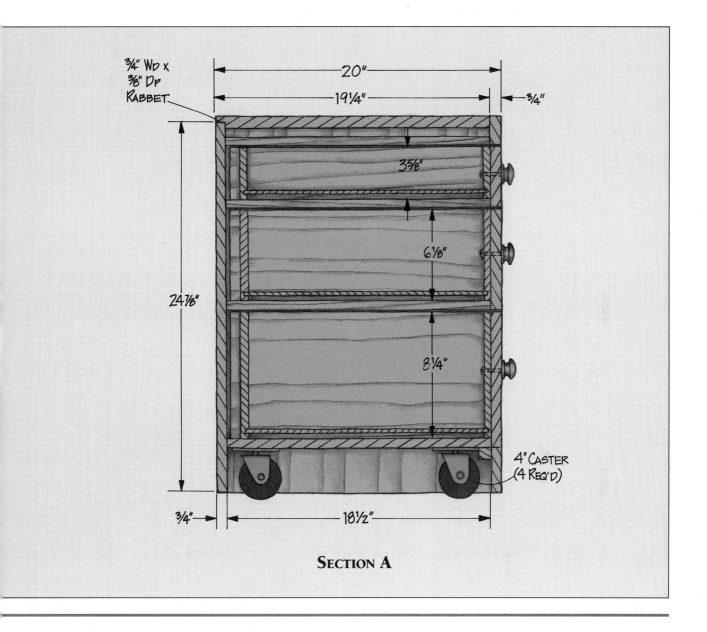

SECTION A

and top edges of the sides to hold the back and top, as shown in the *Side Layout*
- A ³/₄-inch-wide, ³/₈-inch-deep rabbet in the back edge of the top to hold the back, as shown in *Section A*
- ³/₄-inch-wide, ³/₈-inch-deep dadoes in the sides to hold the top shelf and drawer guides

3 Assemble the case. Finish sand the parts of the drawer unit case. Glue the drawer guides in their dadoes in the sides so the front ends of the guides are flush with the front edges of the sides. Also glue the

cleat to the back face of the apron so the top edges of both pieces are flush. Let the glue dry.

Assemble the sides, back, top, and shelf with glue and reinforce the joint with flathead wood screws. Then attach the valance and the apron with glue and screws. Counterbore and countersink all screws, then cover the heads with wooden plugs. Sand the plugs flush with the surrounding surface.

4 Cut the drawer parts to size. No matter how carefully you work, the size of a case sometimes chan-

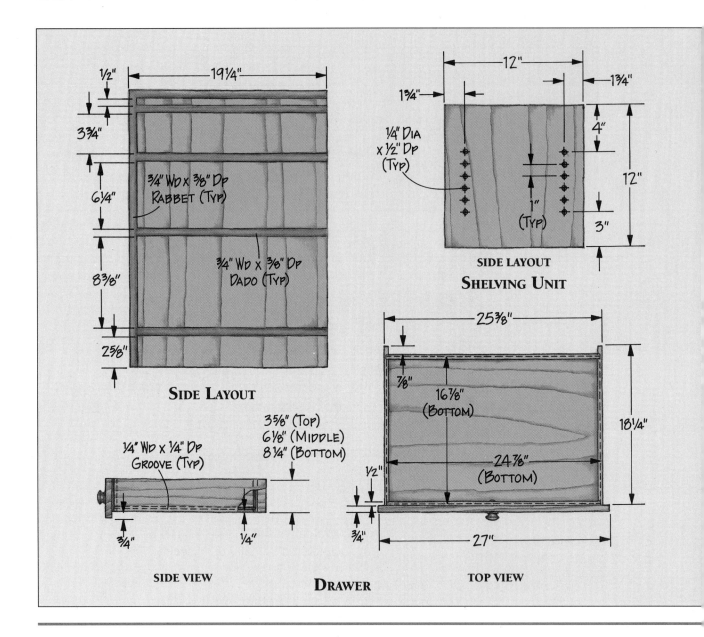

SIDE LAYOUT

½" 19¼"

3¾"

¾" Wᴅ x ⅜" Dᴘ
RABBET (Tʏᴘ)

6¼"

¾" Wᴅ x ⅜" Dᴘ
DADO (Tʏᴘ)

8⅜"

2⅝"

SIDE LAYOUT

12"

1¾"   1¾"

¼" Dɪᴀ
x ½" Dᴘ
(Tʏᴘ)

4"

12"

1"
(Tʏᴘ)

3"

SIDE LAYOUT
SHELVING UNIT

25⅜"

⅞"

16⅞"
(BOTTOM)

18¼"

24⅞"
(BOTTOM)

½"

¾"

27"

¼" Wᴅ x ¼" Dᴘ
GROOVE (Tʏᴘ)

3⅝" (TOP)
6⅛" (MIDDLE)
8¼" (BOTTOM)

¾"   ¼"

SIDE VIEW   **TOP VIEW**
DRAWER

ges as you build it. For this reason, it's best to wait until after you've assembled the case before cutting the drawer parts.

Measure the opening in the front of the case. If it varies from what is shown in the drawings, adjust the sizes of the drawer parts to compensate. Then cut the drawer parts to size.

5 Cut the drawer joinery.   The drawers are assembled with simple rabbets, dadoes, and grooves. Cut these joints:

■ ½-inch-wide, ¼-inch-deep rabbets in the front edges of the drawer sides

■ ½-inch-wide, ¼-inch-deep dadoes in the drawer sides, near the back edges

■ ¼-inch-wide, ¼-inch-deep grooves in the drawer sides, fronts, and backs, near the bottom edges

6 Assemble and fit the drawers.   Lightly sand the drawer parts. Glue the door fronts, backs, and sides together. As you do so, slide the bottoms into their grooves. However, do *not* glue the bottoms in place; let them float in their grooves. Also, do *not* glue the drawer faces to the fronts yet.

Slide the drawers into the case, fitting them between the drawer guides. If any of the drawers bind in the

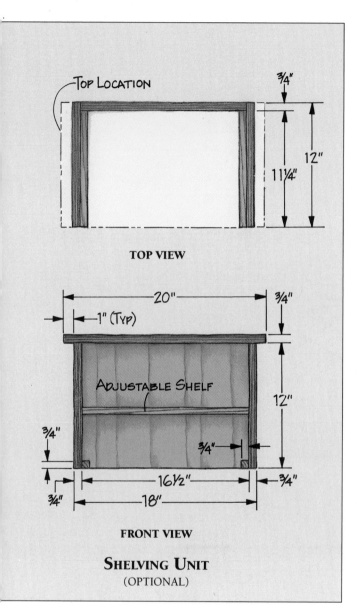

TOP VIEW

FRONT VIEW

SHELVING UNIT
(OPTIONAL)

Remove the drawer faces, spread glue on the drawer fronts, and lay the faces back in place. Temporarily drive #6 flathead wood screws through the pilot holes in the faces and into the fronts — this will hold the faces in place until you can apply the clamps. Remove the drawers from the case and clamp the faces to the drawer fronts. Let the glue dry, then back the screws out of the pilot holes. Enlarge the holes and mount drawer pulls.

MAKING THE SHELVING UNIT

7 **Drill the holes in the shelf.** The adjustable shelf in the shelving unit rests on movable pins, which fit in 1/4-inch-diameter, 1/2-inch-deep holes in the sides. Lay out these holes on the inside faces of the sides, as shown in the *Shelving Unit Side Layout,* then make them with a drill press or a portable drill.

8 **Assemble the shelving unit.** Finish sand the parts of the shelving unit. Assemble the sides, back, and top with glue and flathead wood screws. Then add the cleats, attaching them with glue and screws. As you did before, counterbore and countersink the screws, then cover the heads with plugs. If you wish, cover the edges with veneer strips to hide the exposed plies.

9 **Attach the shelving unit to the drawer unit.** Fasten the shelving unit to the drawer unit by driving flathead wood screws through the shelving cleats and into the drawer unit top. Place shelving support pins into the holes in the sides and lay the adjustable shelf in place.

FINISHING UP

10 **Finish the sharpening station.** Remove the drawers, shelf, and support pins from the case. Do any necessary finish sanding to the wooden surfaces. Apply several coats of tung oil or Danish oil, letting it dry thoroughly between each coat. Rub out the last coat with #0000 steel wool and paste wax — the wax will help the finish resist spills and other abuse. Also wax the drawer guides to help the drawers slide smoothly. Replace the drawers, pins, and shelf.

case, sand or plane the sides until they slide in and out easily. Then remove the drawers and reinforce the rabbet-and-dado joints with wire brads.

Lay the case on its back and place scraps of 1/4-inch plywood on the inside surface of the back, near the corners, to serve as spacers. Slide the drawers all the way into the case — the spacers should hold the drawer fronts flush with the front edges of the case. Place the drawer faces over the fronts, fitting them so there's a 1/32- to 1/16-inch gap between them. Temporarily tape or clamp the faces to the case; then drill 1/8-inch-diameter pilot holes through the faces *and* the fronts where you will later attach drawer pulls.

INDEX

Note: Page references in *italic* indicate photographs or illustrations.
Boldface references indicate charts or tables.

WOODWORKING GLOSSARY

TENON DETAIL

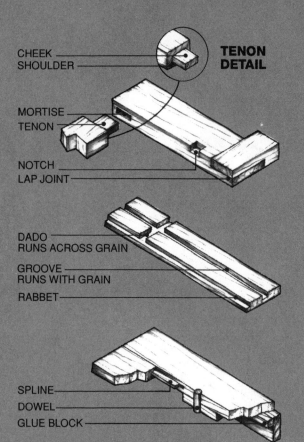

- CHEEK
- SHOULDER
- MORTISE
- TENON
- NOTCH
- LAP JOINT

BASIC JOINERY

- DADO RUNS ACROSS GRAIN
- GROOVE RUNS WITH GRAIN
- RABBET
- SPLINE
- DOWEL
- GLUE BLOCK

FINGER JOINT

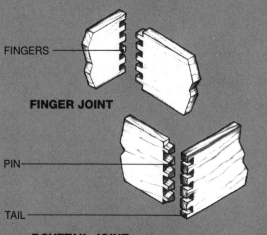

- FINGERS

DOVETAIL JOINT

- PIN
- TAIL

SPECIAL JOINERY

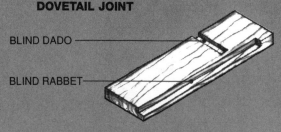

- BLIND DADO
- BLIND RABBET

COMMON SHAPES

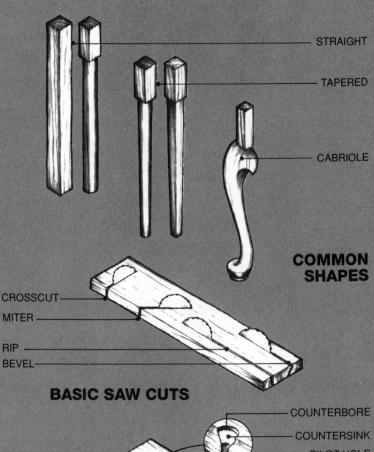

- STRAIGHT
- TAPERED
- CABRIOLE

BASIC SAW CUTS

- CROSSCUT
- MITER
- RIP
- BEVEL

HOLES

- COUNTERBORE
- COUNTERSINK
- PILOT HOLE
- SCREW HOLE
- STOPPED HOLE
- THRU HOLE

PROJECT PLAN SYMBOLS

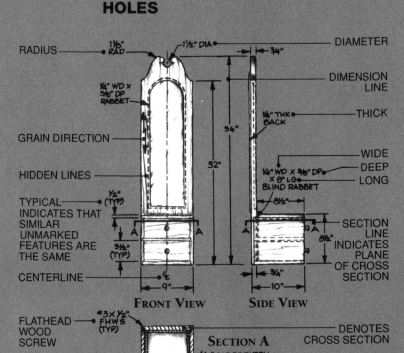

- RADIUS — 1½" RAD
- 1½" DIA — DIAMETER
- ¾"
- ¼" WD x ³⁄₈" DP RABBET
- DIMENSION LINE
- ¼" THK BACK — THICK
- GRAIN DIRECTION
- 36"
- 32"
- ¼" WD X ³⁄₈" DP X 8" LG BLIND RABBET — WIDE / DEEP / LONG
- HIDDEN LINES
- TYPICAL INDICATES THAT SIMILAR UNMARKED FEATURES ARE THE SAME
- ½" (TYP)
- 3½" (TYP)
- 8½"
- SECTION LINE INDICATES PLANE OF CROSS SECTION
- 8½"
- CENTERLINE
- 9"
- ¾"
- 10"

FRONT VIEW **SIDE VIEW**

- FLATHEAD WOOD SCREW — #3 X ½" FHWS (TYP)
- ROUNDHEAD WOOD SCREW — #3 X ½" RHWS

SECTION A
¹⁄₁₆" GAP BETWEEN DRAWER & SIDE

- DENOTES CROSS SECTION

SECTION A